WISE
MOVES

60 Quick Tips to Improve Your Position in Life & Business

GEORGE LUDWIG

CRL
PUBLISHING
GROUP
CHICAGO

Wise Moves

60 Quick Tips to Improve
Your Position in Life & Business

For information:
CRL Publishing Group
2515 Grove Lane
Cary, Illinois 60013-2742 USA

Book design by Ad Graphics, Inc.
Cover photograph by George Papadakis

First printing 2003

ISBN 0-9740223-0-6

Library of Congress Control Number: 2003092103

Although the author and publisher have made every effort to ensure the accuracy and completeness of information contained in this book, we assume no responsibility for errors, inaccuracies, omissions, or any inconsistency herein. Any slights of people, places, or organizations are unintentional.

ATTENTION CORPORATIONS, UNIVERSITIES, COLLEGES, AND PROFESSIONAL ORGANIZATIONS: Special discounts are available on bulk purchases of this book for educational purposes. Book excerpts can also be created to fit specific needs. For information, please contact CRL Publishing Group.

Dedicated to my father,
Charles "Buddha" Ludwig
(1922–2000)

A man who lived wisely

ACKNOWLEDGMENTS

First and foremost, I thank God for giving me the "desire" to live a richer life, a life filled with purpose and passion. The word "desire" in its Latin root means "of the father," so **thanks to God** for desire.

I thank my parents for raising me the right way and for continuing to love me when I went the wrong way. Boy, have I gone the wrong way a few times! An eternal thanks to my father for demonstrating how to live wisely as a man, and to my mother for being such a great role model. I am grateful to my grandmother, Elna Taylor, who always displayed much wisdom around me.

Huge, heartfelt appreciation goes to my sister, editor-in-chief, and writing partner, Sue Ann Burchill, who never wavers in her focus from making sure my writing is always better when it leaves her desk. Thanks, Soup! A big thank-you to my brother-in-law, Tim Burchill, who is a virtual encyclopedia of wisdom, ideas, and illustrations. Tim's insight has often made my work better. Special thanks also to my loving brother and the many friends who have always believed I could somehow pull off my dream of becoming a speaker and author. Big thanks to Becky Keen and Todd Hunt for improving the book with their razor-sharp proofreading skills.

I thank the many mentors who have inspired me to help others break through to greater achievement, fulfillment, prosperity, and happiness. Special thanks to Zig Ziglar, Wayne Dyer, Anthony Robbins, Les Brown, Jim Rohn, Brian Tracy, and my pastors, Bill Hybels and John Ortberg.

Thanks to the many audiences and companies who have listened to me and hired me as I have made my way as a speaker and trainer. I am very grateful to Rita Emmett and Mark Victor Hansen for their support and for being role models to becoming best-selling authors. Thanks also to the many members of the National Speakers Association, both nationally and in Illinois, who have become shock absorbers for me on the rough road to becoming an author. A giant thanks to the entire team at CRL Publishing Group for their tireless work to bring this book to fruition.

Thank you and God Bless you all.

CONTENTS

INTRODUCTION

"Uncle Geo, Uncle Geo, play chess with us. Please, please, please!" one of my 11-year-old twin nephews said, trying to distract me from finishing a speech I was working on.

"The game takes soooo long. I have got to get this work done!" I insisted.

"Just one game, Uncle Geo. We promise we'll play fast," they begged, displaying that childlike persistence that's so hard to deny.

I relented, "Okay, okay, one game, but if you lose, that's it for now. We'll play more tomorrow."

While they set up the board, I grabbed a cup of coffee. I decided that even though I was busy, I would drag the game out a little and let them make a few good captures before I got down to business and checkmated their king. I hadn't played much in recent years, but I had been a proud member of my Junior High School Chess Club. The strategy and tactics used in chess are similar to my approach in teaching peak performance and sales success to corporations, so once I settled in, I was excited about playing. I love the mental competition, the give and take.

"Way to go, you set the board up right. Go ahead and start." I said, sipping a little coffee.

They moved a pawn. I moved a pawn. The game had officially started. What happened in the next few minutes quickly became a blur. They moved. I moved, and then they giggled. When Andrew moved his queen out so quickly, I gave him a chance to redo his move and warned him about risking such a valuable piece so early, but he and Zach just giggled again and said, "No thanks." I moved, and then they moved and giggled. I moved again, and out came their bishop right over to my side of the board.

"Checkmate!" they both shouted and began to laugh hysterically.

"No, that's impossible," I corrected. "You've only made four moves!" But as I scanned the board, I could see they were right, and my king had nowhere to go.

I quickly found out from their mother that they had been going to Chess Club for three months and had also been reading extensively to improve their game. They had learned the *Wise Moves*.

The game of life is no less challenging. We need to know the best moves, the right moves, the wise moves to succeed. Once when I was a high school student and about to depart for a Friday night out, my father asked me, "What time will you be home tonight, son?"

"I should be home by two a.m., Dad," I replied confidently.

"Son, that would not be a wise move!" he responded. "If you want to use the car again, you'll be home by midnight."

Wise moves are the strategies we use that come from intelligent appraisal and discernment of our choices in any situation. They are the actions that lead to positive outcomes, and *Wise Moves* shows us how to apply these in our own lives and businesses. Often we need just a single tip to propel us to the next level personally or professionally.

Unfortunately, we often rely only on our past experience when trying to problem-solve a situation. That experience may have something to teach us, but it can also tie us to old ways of doing and thinking that are no longer effective. Flexibility—a willingness to jettison past strategies that no longer work and to try new solutions—is needed for effective change.

Just as the chief executive officer of a Fortune 100 company keeps looking for ways to change because he or she knows that nothing will be the same in five years, so, too, must you—as the CEO of your own life—always be looking for better ways to do things. If you want to be more successful, you must passionately pursue the discovery of truth and know how to apply that truth appropriately in your life.

That is *wisdom*.

The world is overgorged with information and knowledge—but it is starved for real wisdom. True wisdom is *profound advice*—advice so powerful, and yet so simple, that the minute you use it, it immediately increases the quality of your life.

In short, **Wise Moves** is a book filled with advice for improving your position in life and business. The book is divided into three sections. The first section, *Life Moves,* is a collection of quick tips for increasing the quality of our lives—creating an extraordinary life. The second section, *Sales Moves,* is a collection of sales and marketing tips for increasing sales, expanding business, and achieving greater financial prosperity. The final section, *Life-Changing Quotes,* is a collection of quotes and advice from some of the most influential people of all time. From Oprah Winfrey and Mother Theresa to John F. Kennedy and Zig Ziglar, much can be learned by studying the words of these icons.

If you hunger to improve your life or your business, then turn the page and get reading!

PART I

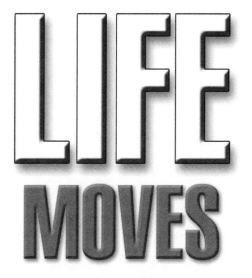

LIFE MOVES

20 Quick Tips to Improve Your Position in Life

1.

One Is a Powerful Number

Don't we often downplay what can be accomplished by just one person? We lose sight of the fact that just one person, with unfailing enthusiasm and consistent industriousness, can achieve results that are truly staggering—a virtual miracle.

As a young man, Elzea Bufier owned a small farm in France where he lived with his wife and only son. He was very content living a simple, peaceful life. Unfortunately tragedy struck, and he lost both his wife and son to sudden illnesses.

Unable to live on his farm without them, he began searching for a new place of solitude. With only his dog and 20 sheep, he roamed the countryside for almost a month. Finally he came upon a spot as desolate as any in France. He found an ancient ruin and decided to make it his new home. The nearest village was over two days' walk, but he decided it was at that spot that he would do his shepherding, so he could live a very quiet, peaceful life.

Even though Elzea was very hurt by his loss, he was still a good man with a giving heart. He decided that somehow he wanted to make a difference in the world in his own quiet way. He had noticed that the land was very barren, without trees. He decided he would remedy that problem by planting a few trees.

As he shepherded by day, he collected acorns from the few sparse oaks that dotted the high country near his new home. Each night after eating his soup, he selected the very best 100 acorns and put them in a pail of water. The next day, when his sheep took their afternoon nap, he would plant the 100 acorns while his dog kept a watchful eye on the sheep.

Every day he planted 100 trees, and by 1913, after just three years of planting, he had planted 100,000 trees. From those 100,000 trees, only 20,000 sprouted. And, from the 20,000 trees that sprouted, only 10,000 survived and grew tall. Yet, even with only a small percentage of his efforts paying off, 10,000 new trees appeared where there had been none before.

Elzea Bufier continued his quiet planting until the day he passed on. For 37 years he had planted at least 100 trees each day. As all the trees grew, nature amplified his miracle. The wind lifted and deposited more seeds which, in turn, drew more moisture and nourished the soil. Where there had once been a desolate, barren countryside, now stood a magnificent forest with a flowing stream and teeming with new life. Eventually, the French Forestry Bureau set aside most of the land as a protected national forest shortly after Bufier peacefully died in 1947.

Elzea Bufier gave the world a great gift. His special service was quiet and unpretentious. He wanted no credit. But his unrelenting enthusiasm and tireless industriousness created a virtual miracle. His story demonstrates the immense impact a single individual can have in the world. He shows us that believing we won't make a difference on our own is just an excuse—one is still a powerful number!

Any Day
Can Be Halloween

Think of the wondrous imagination that fills every child at Halloween. One time he is Hercules, the Olympian, next he is the President of the United States. Another child will be the Statue of Liberty one year and the Princess Pocahontas the next. Adults and children alike enjoy Halloween or Mardi Gras for the very reason that these celebrations give us permission to step outside ourselves and be somebody new. We can do things in our new identities that we would not normally do—things we have always wanted to do but didn't believe we could.

In my Peak Performance Training Workshop, I share a section on the power of our *beliefs*—how they form the foundation for our expectations, attitudes, behaviors, and ultimately, the results we get in our lives. The most important core belief that controls all our perceptions is the belief we have about our Identity. What we can or cannot do, what we consider possible or impossible, is rarely a function of capability, but more often a function of the beliefs we have about who we really are. In addition, the strong need for consistency in our lives causes us to act and behave in accord with our self-view, even when it is not accurate.

When I was growing up, the beliefs I had about my Identity were based on my size. I was the smallest kid in my school, weighing only 112 pounds at graduation. This Identity led to my believing that I could never be an athlete. I also saw myself as timid and afraid of any major challenge or adventure. Through several major life lessons and a lot of difficult self-development work, I began to shift my Identity. Finally, many years later, after overcoming the rejection one experiences during a 20-year sales career, completing two 26-mile marathons, becoming a licensed pilot, and then starting my own business, I know beyond a shadow of a doubt I am not that same person anymore!

Whoever you are reading this right now—and I hope I will get to meet you someday—please know that you have the Power To Reinvent Yourself, no matter how old you are, by simply deciding you can! Decide what beliefs you want to hold about yourself and then develop a plan of action that will bring them to fruition. Today can be your Halloween—the day you put on a new costume or simply let your "real self" shine through! Like Clark Kent, the mild-mannered reporter, shedding his business suit to reveal the mighty Superman, we can all uncover a new Identity that is more than our past, more than our present behaviors, and more than any current label we have been giving ourselves! Trick or Treat, and may your bag be filled to the top!

Discipline:
The Critical Denominator

This year can be our most successful year ever if we are willing to practice more discipline than we ever have before in pursuing our goals. In fact, we will never perform at our very best until we become super self-disciplined. Richard Shelly Taylor, in his book *The Disciplined Life,* defines self-discipline as "the ability to regulate conduct by principle, value, and judgment rather than by impulse, desire, high pressure, or social custom." Discipline is about doing what is necessary, when it is necessary, whether we feel like it or not.

All management is the act of doing what's most important, day-by-day, moment-by-moment. Great management starts with discipline—the execution of putting first things first. Self-mastery comes from self-managing yourself by subordinating the less important actions and disciplining yourself to do the things that really matter right when they need to be done.

There is a great essay by E.M. Gray titled, "The Common Denominator of Success." He spent his life searching for the one denominator that all successful people have. He found that it was not hard work, good luck, or great communication skills, though those were all important. One habit seemed to transcend all the others. "The successful person has the habit of doing the things the others do not like to do," he observed. "Successful people do not necessarily like doing them either, but they subordinate their dislikes to the strength of their purpose." They use their discipline, their independent will, to develop the habits that will guarantee their success.

Gary Player, one of golf's greatest players, has won a large number of major tournaments. Once, when being interviewed, he said, "Throughout my career people have said to me, 'I'd give anything to hit a golf ball like you.'" Gary, who has always been known for being polite and dignified, said that on one particularly tough day, his politeness failed him when a spectator again said, "I would give anything to hit a golf ball like you." Gary said he lost it and responded, "No you wouldn't! You would give anything to hit a golf ball like me IF IT WAS EASY. Do you know what you have to go through to hit a golf ball like me? You've got to get up every morning at five o'clock, go out to the course, and hit 1,000 balls. Your hands start bleeding; you walk back to the clubhouse, wash the blood off, slap on a bandage, and then go out and hit another 1,000 balls. That's what it takes to hit a golf ball like me." Player was demonstrating the single, most critical, common denominator of all successful people—DISCIPLINE. If we follow his lead, this year can be our most successful year ever!

Fly Straight to Your Destination:
Watch Your Habit-Heading Indicator

My flight instructor Steve McFadden yelled, "Watch your Heading Indicator!" It was when I was first learning to fly, that Steve noticed that I had let the Heading Indicator drift from a heading of 080 to 081. I said, "Steve, chill out! We're only off by one degree." Out of a total of 360 degrees, like a compass, one degree didn't seem like very much. Steve quickly gave me an education as he explained that one degree might not mean much for a few miles, but as the distance increased, even one degree off would eventually put us way off course. Steve taught me one of aviation's most critical navigation lessons—that you must constantly monitor your heading to stay on course. Winds aloft, airspace restrictions, air traffic control directions, laziness, and several other factors can distract a pilot, resulting in the airplane being off of its correct heading.

When we strive to reach personal goals, we also need to stay on course. Habits are the tools we use to do so. Jack Canfield, co-author of *The Power of Focus*, makes the case that 90% of our normal behavior is based on our habits. Most of our daily activities are simply routines. We all have habits for our dress, our health, our diet, our work, our income, our relationships, and much more. For example, if our goal is to lose 12 pounds in six months and at the end of two months we've lost only one pound, then it's obvious our Habit-Heading Indicator is indicating we're off course. The sooner we correct the habits needed to stay on course, the greater the chance we can arrive at the destination we set out to reach. While being a little off course does not seem like much of a problem in the short term, pretty soon we discover that, just as with flying, small problems with our habitual behavior prevent us from reaching our destination.

The first key is to identify which habits are necessary to reach the goals we have set. For the salesperson, it may be the number of calls per day; for the runner, it may be how many miles run per week; and for the mother, it may be how much time to allow for the children to watch TV. The second key is to relentlessly monitor our Habit-Heading Indicator so that the needle stays centered right on our desired goal. Discipline and commitment are needed to prevent distractions from pulling us off course. The third and final key is to quickly make corrections when we have determined that our habits have slipped and pulled us off course. Even if our habits have us off by only one degree, we must remember how Steve explained that things would get much worse if we do not make immediate corrections. If we can keep the needle centered on our goals, we will enjoy a fantastic flight.

5.

Get the Hunger PANG

The word *kaizen* means "constant and never-ending improvement" in Japanese. There is no pursuit more noble or important than the pursuit of self-improvement. Consistent and constant enrichment in all areas of your life is essential to reaching your true potential. I developed an acronym for this called PANG, which stands for Perpetual And Never-ending Growth. All Peak Performers seem committed to daily improvement in both their personal and professional lives. Michael Jordan, Tiger Woods, Mahatma Gandhi, Nelson Mandela, and Oprah Winfrey all have the personal trademark of improving themselves daily. Their commitment to the philosophy of PANG means they both hunger for success and continually raise their standards to attain greater success. Small daily improvements—whether spending some time exercising, reading, visualizing, or strengthening relationships—become like regular deposits into your Peak Performance bank account. Over time, even in a single year, you will enjoy the effect of compounded interest. Very soon your bank account called Peak Performance will make you a very wealthy person in all facets of life!

6.

He Who Laughs, Lasts!

Humor is a powerful tool for our lives, particularly during difficult times. Most of the top business executives and achievers I have met seem to all have a great sense of humor. They seem to know that a happy heart and lots of laughter are critical for both their professional and personal success. They work hard, but also recognize the value of using humor to gain perspective during serious situations. Laughter is a great survival skill for relieving tension and allowing us to handle the constant change that is all too present in today's business environment.

Corporate layoffs and a stumbling economy have most people working longer than ever before just to keep up. So much stress has been created that record numbers of people are breaking down on the road of life. *The Wall Street Journal* reports that employment disability claims have doubled in the past 10 years and that 46% of Americans describe their jobs as highly stressful. In fact, 34% considered quitting their jobs due to stress, and 14% actually did quit. Working in today's business climate is taking its toll on everybody's health and sanity.

C.W. Metcalf, in his book *Lighten Up: Survival Skills for People Under Pressure*, urges business leaders and CEOs to infuse humor into the workplace. He says, "Humor is the survival skill that relieves tension, keeping us fluid and flexible instead of becoming rigid and breakable, in the face of relentless change." It lightens our load by preventing us from taking ourselves too seriously and gives us a healthier perspective on the challenges we face.

Many resources are available to help you bring more humor into your life. Psychiatric nurse and fellow speaker Donna Strickland, who conducts seminars around the country on the importance of humor in the workplace, has developed the quintessential compilation entitled *A How-To Primer to Stimulate More Humor in the Workplace*. Donna says, "We need humor and laughter to develop a thankful, grateful heart about life. Humor helps us down that road."

In addition, Tim Hansel's book, *You Gotta Keep Dancin'*, has many thoughts to get you laughing. He reminds you that you're having a bad day if...

1. You call your answering service and they tell you it's none of your business.

2. You put your pants on backward—and they fit better.

3. Your horn goes off accidentally and remains stuck as you follow a group of Hell's Angels down the highway.

4. You sink your teeth into a fabulous filet mignon and they stay there.

Humor not only helps us deal with work-related stress, but even helps us recover from illnesses. The act of laughing actually produces a series of physiological reactions (such as altered endocrine levels) that promote improved health. Norman Cousins pioneered the healing benefits of humor by literally laughing his way back to health after being struck with cancer. His daily routine consisted of immersing himself in films, TV programs, and books that made him laugh. His book *Anatomy of an Illness* shares the amazing way in which this regimen led to a complete recovery.

Take time to laugh along the road of life because he who laughs, lasts! Where can we find a laugh? Humor is everywhere if we just keep our eyes open for it. Business humorist Todd Hunt reminds us that we only have to look at some of the ridiculous signs all around us in businesses to get a good chuckle. He shares one he discovered recently in one of our nation's largest hardware chains. The sign read: CASHIERS ARE NOT ALLOWED TO MAKE CHANGE. You have to wonder...what good are they then?

7

Unhabitual Thinking:
The Key to Genius

"Genius...means little more than the faculty of perceiving in an unhabitual way," wrote William James, considered by many to be the father of American psychology. Peak Performers think "outside the lines" or "outside the box." The greatest ally of mediocrity is habitual thinking. By midlife, we have all acquired a long list of habits, some good and some bad, to help us organize our lives. Most routines we develop make our lives easier and are therefore a blessing. Some habits, though, keep us from reaching our full potential. We have all heard the cliché about the man who, though he worked for the company for 30 years, really had only one year of experience repeated 30 times. Peak Performers shed the bad habits that are holding them back from great accomplishments.

Roger Bannister was the epitome of overcoming habitual thinking. Running the mile in less than four minutes had been deemed a physically impossible feat. Many tried; no one could do it. Even the Greeks, who had tied runners to horses for such an attempt, could not master this impossible barrier. Someone forgot to tell that to Roger Bannister, however. On May 6, 1954 in Oxford, England, Roger screamed around the last lap to finish with a time of 3:59.4. By thinking "outside the lines," Roger became the first human being to ever run a mile in less than four minutes.

This isn't the end of the story, however. Within a month, John Landry also ran a less-than-four-minute mile and within a year

12 other runners had done so. Once the barrier of habitual thinking had been broken, people realized it was a psychological barrier and not a physical one. It was only habitual thinking. Thank God for Roger Bannister and all the men and women determined to be unhabitual thinkers! They are the Peak Performers in life, which William James labeled genius.

8.

Take the First Step:
How to Break Through Any Fear

During a recent workshop I led called *The Bold Zone*, I asked for an audience volunteer to participate in an exercise that demonstrates one of the major keys for beating fear. Most experts agree that fear, conscious or unconscious, is what keeps us from venturing out to try new activities, new work ideas, new careers, and even new relationships. We must break through fear to experience the maximum amount of joy, growth, and success that life has available for all of us.

Shirley P., a 51-year-old female, came to the stage as our nervous volunteer. She identified her goal as wanting to lead a healthier life and lose weight, but she knew that her fear of physical exercise, being seen in a gym or in workout clothes, sweating, or participating in sports of any kind prevented her from achieving this.

I told Shirley that she would soon be able to demonstrate that anyone can break a 1" by 12" piece of wood with their bare hands. Board breaking is a good metaphor for teaching people how to unleash their power and overcome their fears. When I poll audience members, over 90% usually doubt that they could break a board—it is definitely way outside their zone of comfort. The experience of achieving something outside our comfort zone or believed abilities (in this case, breaking a board) shows us we can tackle other intimidating situations in our lives as well.

Shirley and I then listed all of her fears, related both to breaking the board and starting her physical exercise program on one side of the pine board. On the other side, we listed her desire for a better body and better health, and her goals for losing weight.

We also wrote that one of her goals was to break the board, so that she could leave with the strong memory of her triumph over fear.

Next I helped Shirley to emotionally link the positive feelings that come with better health, a more attractive body, and higher self-esteem to the event of actually breaking the board. Conversely, we associated the pain of gaining weight or never getting healthy with not breaking the board. This helped give Shirley a strong enough reason to believe she MUST break the board.

Shirley also needed her most resourceful physiology to accomplish this goal, so we cranked up the music and got the whole audience dancing to get her in a high-energy peak state. Then I had her hold up the piece of wood and repeat a few affirmations loudly and with emotion—affirmations such as "I Will Break the Wood! I Will Beat My Fear! I Will Be Fit! I Will Be Healthy! I Will Be Powerful!"

Shirley was ready to face her fear and break the board. She definitely WANTED to make some changes, and she saw the board as a symbol for her new beginning. I asked her if she was scared and she replied, "Yes, and I am not sure I can do it!" As I stood holding the wood, she looked it over carefully and with increasing doubt. I said, "Shirley, you don't have to be 100% certain. You just need to have enough faith to take that first punch. TAKE THAT FIRST STEP!"

Shirley's hesitation reminded me of the climax of the movie *Indiana Jones and the Last Crusade*. Indiana was facing one of the supremely difficult tests needed to reach the Holy Grail and save his dying father. Indiana comes to the edge of a large chasm— about 100 feet across and 1,000 feet down. On the other side of the chasm is the doorway to the Holy Grail. The instructions say, "Only in a leap from the lion's head, will he prove his worth."

Indiana says to himself, "It's impossible. Nobody can jump this." Then he realizes that this test requires a leap of faith. His father says, "You must believe, boy. You must believe!" Even though every nerve and fiber of Indiana's being was scared and telling him to quit, Indiana walks to the edge of the cliff… lifts his foot… and then steps out into the thin air.

Shirley began to take a few practice punches toward the board but appeared more scared then ever. Even I, the self-acclaimed expert, began to worry that she might back out. She hesitated just like Indiana Jones did before he stepped out into thin air—and found himself held up by an invisible bridge. He just took that first step and beat the fear.

How much faith do WE need to break through our fears? Here's the good news—we do not need perfect certainty. Indiana Jones had a cavern full of fear and uncertainty, as was evident by the beads of sweat on his forehead, yet all he needed was enough faith to take that first step.

Shirley took her first step, too, and let out a loud and forceful Ki-Hap (yell) before blasting her right hand, palm up, right through the board! As I stood there holding the two pieces of wood, Shirley screamed, "I did it! I did it! I can't believe I did it!" Next she gave me a big hug just as the audience stood up to applaud her.

Shirley had discovered what Indiana Jones already knew, that a critical key for breaking through any fear and going beyond our zone of comfort is to simply have enough faith to TAKE THAT VERY FIRST STEP.

9

Peak Performers Focus on Winning

Peak Performers do not dwell on their mistakes. Great performers always find a way to focus on only what's necessary to be victorious. A few years ago Michael Jordan did a commercial for Nike in which he recounted some of his failures: "I've missed over 9,000 shots in my career, lost over 300 games, and 26 times I took the game-winning shot at the buzzer and missed." Jordan was later interviewed about whether he had really missed that many shots. Jordan's response was revealing: "I have no idea." People were disappointed by the comment, but it revealed a key to his personality. Michael Jordan did not dwell on his past mistakes. Michael Jordan dwelled on what he could do at that moment to guarantee his team's victory. Peak Performers dwell on winning and keep their minds off past mistakes.

10.

Power Physiology: The Bold Route to Rapid Results

Did you know that your physiology is the most powerful tool you have to instantly change your emotional state of being and bring about new, outstanding results? It is our biggest leverage, because it works so fast and without fail. If we change our posture, breathing, muscle tension, and tonality, we instantly change our state. Simple and easily controlled physiology, such as our facial expressions, can put us in the state where we develop the same certainty Michael Jordan and Tiger Woods have as they pursue their goals. I call this "THE BOLD STATE"—that state of unstoppable passion—where we have an excited sense of certainty about ourselves and our goals.

You might be surprised to know that my seminars involve lots of organized yelling, loud music, raucous laughter, and a joyful frenzy. I instruct participants to chant "I am BOLD," jump up and down, dance, clap, shake their fists like Rocky, strut like peacocks—whatever it takes to act as if they were totally energized. One major way to achieve any outcome is to act "as if" you were already more powerful, resourceful, and certain that you'll succeed. Acting "as if" effectively puts your physiology in the state you need to be in to accomplish your goals. I help my clients access their most dynamic, vital, and excited physiology, because no powerful actions come without a powerful state to operate from!

Physiology creates choices that lead to results. The reason people take drugs, drink alcohol, drink coffee, or smoke cigarettes is because they want to indirectly change their state by changing their physiology. My workshops teach ways we can change our state in a far more constructive manner—and we condition them on the spot, like doing extra weight-lifting curls for a bicep muscle. Remember, you can—ZAP!—change your state in an instant by changing your physiology. I encourage you to access your BOLD STATE and enjoy the passion and RESULTS you deserve on your journey as a Peak Performer!

11.

Is Your Nose Growing?

Arthur Andersen, Enron, WorldCom, and Martha Stewart are all news stories that have been linked to some sort of unethical behavior. As taxpayers, you and I fund massive Justice Department expenditures in trying to determine who, if anyone, is telling the truth in these messy cases of economic greed.

It's a shame that the Italian writer Carlo Lorenzini's symbol of dishonesty, Pinocchio's growing nose, was only real in his 19th century fairy tale. Wouldn't it be great if these corporate executives' noses would lengthen whenever they lied? We could resolve corporate America's ethics violations more easily, more quickly, and more economically.

Surveys cited in business magazines and management books confirm that both employees and employers site the personal characteristic of honesty as the number-one trait they value. When single people describe their perfect partner, they inevitably say they want an honest man or woman who can be trusted in every way. Above all, everyone wants to be dealt with truthfully.

Then if we all agree that honesty is so important, how do we end up with so many corporations misleading their clients and stockholders? As a seminar leader, I meet many people who share with me that their life is not working out. They talk to me about their broken dreams, faded hopes, and thwarted goals. In many cases, when they really open up, and we trace their disappointments back far enough, we often find a trail of dishonesty. In an effort to present ourselves as just a little bit better or smarter or more accomplished, we often depart from the absolute truth a tiny bit. It's easy to rationalize away the importance of these "stretches of truth," but they gradually lead to an erosion of our character. Bit by bit, we've traded away who we really are for a vision of something that looks good but isn't real. Eventually we're exposed, the world sees our $3.9B accounting "error," prospects will no longer trust us enough to give us their business, and someone has finally noticed that our noses are a lot longer than everyone else's.

If we want to take honesty seriously, we need to realize what it means in terms of ourselves and how we conduct our business with others. Being honest involves becoming transparent and letting others see us as we really are. What we give up in this approach is the ability to make things seem better than they are, which may be a leverage we've often used in closing a sale. What we gain, however, is the confidence of our clients because they know who we truly are and that they can trust and rely upon what we say. Our task is to gain back the trust that Enron, WorldCom, and others have lost.

In the old fairy tale, Pinocchio lied so much that his nose grew to such a great length that he could not get through a doorway. Being honest keeps open the door of trust that is necessary to have healthy relationships, both personal and professional.

12.

How to Reach Your Goals

It always seems easier to set a goal than to follow it through to completion. For example, we've all tried improving ourselves—whether by losing weight, quitting smoking, improving our relationships, attaining career objectives, or achieving financial goals. Excited at the outset, we imagine our worthy outcome and feel eager to achieve it. Our goals seem so reachable.

But then it happens—we lose the motivation to reach our goals. We let the day's commitment slide, and our dedication wanes. With our resolve lost or weakened, we become mired in our old patterns and ultimately discouraged. Sound familiar? I've been there, and you probably have too.

Any day can start a new year for us. And even though we can't get a brand new start in life, we can start now and ensure a brand new ending. We can begin to create the quality of life we desire when we admit we are not where we want to be. General Norman Schwarzkopf said it best when he said, "Change is always impossible until the moment we are willing to acknowledge that things are not yet perfect." The greatest achievers acknowledge a gap between where they are and where they want to be.

An easy recipe for creating an outstanding year and embarking on an extraordinary life journey can be found in the simple metaphor of getting three "A's" and one "C" on an imaginary school report card.

The first A you need stands for ACTION PLAN. Once you know what your goal is for the year and why you want it, you'll need an ACTION PLAN to determine what you must do in order to achieve it. When your outcome is clearly defined and the steps for reaching it plainly laid out, the emotional drive necessary for its accomplishment will be present. Most people don't fail because they planned on failing; they fail because they failed to plan at all. Your first A is for ACTION PLAN.

The second A you need stands for ATTITUDE. Even with a brilliant action plan, you still need a great ATTITUDE to reach your goals. Legend has it that football coach Vince Lombardi's Green Bay Packers were having a bad season one year. Lombardi brought the team into the locker room after a practice. He stressed the relationship between the team's attitude and the win-loss record. Lombardi said, "Fellas, your abilities say 'win,' but your attitudes say 'lose.'" Lombardi knew there is really very little difference among abilities of high-level athletes, but very big differences in mental attitude, which in turn led to big differences in the win-loss columns. History's greatest achievements have been made by people who excelled only slightly over the other people in their fields, but who had an edge by virtue of their attitudes. So the second A you need on your report card is ATTITUDE.

The third A you must have stands for ACTIVITY LEVEL. Let me stress the fact that the most intelligent, strategic, and workable plan for attaining your goals won't work—if *you* won't. Work is the price we enjoy to travel the road to our goals. We can guard best against losing our shirts by keeping our sleeves rolled up. We have to make the sales calls, study the lessons, heal the patients, teach the children, find the criminals, or do whatever activities are needed to get us closer to our goals. We must put in extra effort, extra enthusiasm, extra loyalty, and extra hours if we want to reach our objectives. In a nutshell, if we go the extra mile, we will ultimately reach our destination.

Now with three A's on our imaginary report card, we've almost made the honor roll. But surprisingly, we also need a C on the report card if we want to guarantee reaching our goals. The C is our insurance policy for achieving the objective. C stands for COACHING. No matter how committed we are or how much willpower we have, we all need a COACH who cares and who has the skills to challenge us to step up and maximize the quality of our lives—with conscious thought, decision, and action.

In my life, I have searched for COACHES to assist me in finding those small distinctions or strategies that can save years of time, energy, or frustration. I have also needed them to hold me accountable to the commitments I made to myself. As the beneficiary of great COACHING, I eventually became a pretty great coach myself. I've been fortunate enough to consult and coach a wide variety of people, including salespeople, entrepreneurs, nurses, professional speakers, corporate leaders, and construction workers.

And here's what my experiences have taught me: No matter what a person's status or level of achievement in society, those who have reached the pinnacle of success in life do not rest on their laurels once they've reached the top. They keep striving for more. They are hungry. And, like you and me, their hunger invariably causes them to seek out the finest resources and the best COACHES to help them attain even greater levels of fulfillment. Life's greatest achievers—like Michael Jordan, Tiger Woods, Warren Buffet, and even Bill Gates—utilize coaching to keep closing the gap between where they are and where they want to be.

The COACHING system I developed is modeled after the very best in the world and is now being used to help serious achievers attain phenomenal results. The One-on-One Rapid Results Coaching System keeps the focus, training, and accountability front and center—where it must be—to guarantee that we reach our goals.

Whether you choose the Rapid Results Coaching System, obtain professional coaching from another source, or find a special mentor who will coach you, coaching provides the necessary bridge to reaching your objectives.

Remember that it takes three "A's" and one "C" on the imaginary report card to reach our goals this year and make the Honor Roll of Life. A great ACTION PLAN, the right ATTITUDE, an extra-high ACTIVITY LEVEL, and some outstanding COACHING will speed us down the highway toward our goals, and put us in the fast lane toward a great life!

13.

Go Back to School,
but Don't Forget Your Brain

Whether you're going "back to school" officially, or continuing your self-education in the school of life, you must not forget your brain! This obviously most important part of the body for learning requires care that might not always be so apparent. It needs three essentials to maximize its potential and make you a Peak Learner: exercise, rest, and nutrition.

Your brain weighs in at only 2% of your body's weight, yet it consumes 25% of your oxygen intake. When a person's oxygen supply is shut off, even for a few minutes, brain cells begin to die. Oxygen is the single most important nutrient the 75 trillion cells of the body need to thrive or even survive. Oxygen will energize the brain so that better learning can take place. For these reasons, regular exercise in the middle of learning sessions is highly advisable. Everything from reading to attending a workshop should be interrupted by deep breathing and brisk movement at the very least.

Adequate rest is also important. Having consistent sleeping patterns will result in optimum brain functioning for most people. Disrupting your customary sleep habits will result in reduced mental alertness and acuity, as is often seen with jet lag. The amount of sleep needed has been shown to vary by the individual, but recent research suggests that most Americans suffer from some degree of sleep deprivation.

Finally, nutrition plays a major role in the functioning of your brain. Just as the brain uses the lion's share of the oxygen intake, the brain is also exceptionally sensitive to diet. It is very difficult to learn something after a big meal, such as a Thanksgiving feast, because the body's blood supply is tied up in digestion, leaving very little available to carry the oxygen necessary for alert learning. Many nutritionists counsel on the benefits of eating a well-balanced, healthy diet, stressing the importance of lots of fruit and vegetables, and a reduction in processed foods. Cutting back on alcohol, sugar, caffeine, starch, and drugs also contributes to a healthier lifestyle.

Finding a nutritional strategy to immediately improve one's mental sharpness for peak learning sessions is very valuable. My own experimentation in this area has yielded several keys to top performance. I have found that different foods create "ups and downs" because of shifts in my brain chemistry. Carbohydrates make me sleepy, protein adds alertness, and fat slows me down mentally. By minimizing carbohydrates, eating lightly, consuming lean protein, drinking green power drinks, increasing my water intake, and using caffeine in moderation, I can produce the most positive and alert brain state. If you will exercise regularly, rest properly, and follow good nutritional practices, you really can go back to school without forgetting your brain!

14.

Fill 'er Up with Love

I remember as a kid, growing up in Indiana, going to our local gas station where the owner knew my parents. We would pull in and be greeted by the heavyset proprietor, named Toby, doing a high-speed waddle to our car. He always asked, "Fill 'er up, Bud?" with a big, toothy grin, to which my dad always replied, "Yes sir, Toby!" Toby would then begin his normal ritual of pumping the gas, washing the windows, and checking the oil and tire pressure. He never forgot to stop and talk with my dad, look him in the eye, smile, ask him how we all were, and offer a kind compliment. He would invite me into the station, where I always acted surprised to receive a Buffalo-head nickel. I loved going there so much to see Toby, hear his big laugh, and of course get a nickel, which was a lot of cash for a seven-year-old in 1964. My dad was always in a better mood after we left Toby's gas station—it was as if he got filled up too!

I have often thought about those trips to the gas station. We all desperately need to be filled up on a daily basis with what Toby was dispensing. Toby was filling people up with love. Toby knew that putting in long hours at work, parenting, or at school drains your emotional tank dry. Toby also knew that financial, health, and relationship challenges can leave your tank empty! We are all designed to need frequent refueling of our emotional tanks by family and friends so we don't break down on the road of life.

Toby knew that we can't fill our own tanks, only someone else's. He practiced a philosophy that we can all use to top off the tank of a family member, a friend, a coworker, or even a stranger.

Toby's method was tied to doing three simple things:

1. The Look
2. The Words
3. The Touch

Toby could make you feel better just by LOOKING you in the eye and smiling to make you feel his love and genuine warmth. Toby always had a kind WORD or compliment to make you feel special, unique, and happy. Toby would also always shake your hand, or TOUCH your forearm, or squeeze your shoulder in a way that made you feel really good. Toby, without a formal education, already knew what the psychologists have long been studying—that human beings need to be touched on a daily basis.

We often encounter people whose tanks are dry. Remember to use the look, the words, and the touch to help someone FILL 'ER UP!

15.

You've Got to Pay the Price

Several years ago, I had just finished eating my favorite steamed dish at a nearby Chinese restaurant and was walking outside, when the owner came running out shouting, "Hey Mister! You've Got to Pay the Price." You see, my mind being elsewhere, I had left the restaurant without paying my bill! Later I realized the incident really resonates with a unique truth about a life of achievement.

In one sense, we can choose almost anything we want from the menu of life, and we'll be able to get it. But in another sense, there are times when we're going to have to pay first, before we can get what we ordered. We have to pay the price BEFORE we'll be able to enjoy the great taste of what we've selected from the menu of life.

Knowing what we want out of life is critical, but it's not enough to make our dreams come true. Longing for something is not enough to guarantee we will obtain it. I believe that when it comes to fulfilling our dreams, there is always a price we must pay, and most of the time that price needs to be paid "up front."

We live in a culture that promotes a "quick fix" mentality for reaching our goals. Gone are the words "patience," "sacrifice," "perseverance," "work," "diligence," and "duty." They have been replaced with "I want it all, and I want it now!" Wealth, relationships, and health are expected without any struggle or wait. People see a new sports car and want it now, despite the fact they cannot afford it. Relationships flourish and fail faster than paint can dry. No one seems willing to delay their gratification—they want to get the best dish on the menu when they want it, whether they can afford it or not. That may be human nature, but it isn't necessarily how life works.

But…if we're willing to apply ourselves, work hard, be patient, and sacrifice, we really *can* achieve our goals. It will not happen overnight, but it will happen. I know, being self-employed, that there is a tremendous amount of sweat equity involved. Most experts agree it takes three to five years just to lay a good foundation. I've seen many people quit their business because they got tired of paying the price, right at the point of finally achieving real success.

Renowned ice climber Yvon Chouinard became a blacksmith to invent the perfect ice ax for his fellow climbers. But even as Chouinard's reputation grew throughout the nation as the only individual making unique equipment for climbers, he had to sell his wares from the trunk of his dilapidated car, surviving on cans of cat food he bought by the case. With time, diligence, and immense sacrifice, Yvon Chouinard now has a $50 million business selling what many consider the premier outdoor equipment in the world today. Yvon's life demonstrates this major principle of success—first we pay the price, and then we get to savor the very best entrées from the menu of life.

16.

Get in Flow:
Create Rich Life Experiences

I popped up out of the azure blue Mediterranean ocean on a slalom water-ski, with the breath-taking city Monte Carlo serving as my picture-perfect backdrop. My full attention was focused on the movements of my body, the ski, the salty air whistling past my face, and the gorgeous scenery flying by. There was no room in my mind for conflicts or confusion. I knew that any distraction could easily lead to a face plant on one of the ocean's waves. But I didn't want to get distracted anyway! The ski run was so perfect, I wanted it to go on forever…I wanted to stay totally immersed in that awesome experience for as long as I could. I was getting in the FLOW.

If waterskiing doesn't mean much to you, then substitute one of your favorite passions in this vignette. It could be dancing, cooking, writing, working on the computer, reading a good book, or even working in your garden. Or it could be when you're immersed in a complicated kitchen remodeling project or a very competitive business deal. Or it could occur when you're playing with your baby or just "hanging out" in the moment with close friends. In moments like these, contrary to much of our everyday lives, what we feel, what we wish, and what we think are in total harmony.

Mihaly Csikszentmihalyi, author of the book *Flow*, uses the metaphor FLOW to describe that sense of effortless action. Athletes refer to this as "being in the zone," and artists often call this "aesthetic rapture."

Csikszentmihalyi discovered that FLOW usually occurs when a person faces a clear set of goals that require predictable responses. Playing chess, playing tennis or a musical piece, weaving a rug, climbing a mountain—all tend to induce FLOW. They all create a little self-contained universe where it's possible to pursue the goal without questioning what should be done next. This clarity of what is needed to achieve the goal tends to induce the state of optimal experience.

He also found that FLOW is more likely to occur when a person's skills are fully engaged in overcoming a challenge that requires all of our resources but doesn't overwhelm us. Taking on gradually increasing challenges, and then learning the necessary skills to meet those challenges, creates an environment where FLOW is very likely to occur. "Flow Experiences" provide flashes of intense living that bring our physical and psychic energies into harmony and create a richness of living.

Finally, after being totally exhausted, I dropped the ski handle and slipped into the water to wait for the water-ski tow boat to return and pick me up. As I climbed onto the boat's platform, handed them my ski, and gazed at my surroundings, an incredible feeling of fulfillment crept over me. If we engage in the activities we love—those for which we've set clear goals, those which provide relevant feedback, and those for which we're committed to improving our skills—then we'll be setting ourselves up to experience FLOW more frequently in our lives. And the more we get in FLOW, the richer our lives become.

Leadership 101: Integrity by Example

Integrity comes from a congruence among thoughts, feelings, words, and actions—when all that you are and do springs from your core values. Gandhi was one of the greatest examples of integrity we have seen in modern times, and the many moving stories about his life demonstrate the power of teaching this character trait by example.

A mother once brought her child, asking him to tell the young boy not to eat sugar, because it was not good for his diet or his developing teeth. Gandhi replied, "I cannot tell him that. But you may bring him back in a month." The mother was angry as Gandhi moved on, brushing her aside. She had traveled some distance, and had expected the mighty leader to support her parenting. She had little recourse, so she left for her home. One month later she returned, not knowing what to expect. The great Gandhi took the small child's hands into his own, knelt before him, and tenderly communicated, "Do not eat sugar, my child. It is not good for you." Then he embraced him and returned the boy to his mother. The mother, grateful but perplexed, queried, "Why didn't you say that a month ago?" "Well," said Gandhi, "a month ago, I was still eating sugar." What power in example!

This rare kind of integrity has great power. Imagine what the world would be like if all present-day leaders of nations had that kind of integrity. What if we could depend on their word in any situation? What if trust and confidence were the foundation of every business relationship? Because of his integrity, millions trusted Gandhi; millions learned from him and counted themselves as his followers. Collectively, they became a force strong enough to gain political independence for India. True leaders demonstrate Integrity by Example.

18

Give a Priceless Gift: Encouraging Words Change Lives

In 1979, after serving 30 days in jail for a drug conviction and struggling to restart my life, I desperately wanted to get a better job than the one I had at McDonald's. I spotted an employment ad for a car salesperson at Hefner Chevrolet in Fort Wayne, Indiana. My friends convinced me that it would be a waste of time to apply because I had no sales experience, no great knowledge of cars, and no college degree. Then one day, shortly before Christmas in 1979, my dad gave me a present: a handmade coupon to buy a suit with a note attached. It read, "You can't hit a ball you don't take a swing at. Go for the Hefner job, son, you might get a hit." I got that job, and in doing so, took a major step toward rebuilding my character and my life.

Each of us goes through a time when we're at a crossroads and not sure what to do next. Then someone comes along and says just the right words to get us through it. Perhaps it's something our parents or a teacher says. Or maybe we read it in a book, hear it at a seminar, or pull it from a song. But the words change our lives and often remain with us forever.

When Shaquille O'Neal was a teenager at a summer basketball camp, he didn't think he measured up to the other players. He told his mother he would try harder next year, but she said, "Do your best now. Later doesn't always come for everybody." Shaquille never forgot those words, and they built a work ethic which led to him being one of the greatest players in the game.

While actions often speak louder than words, words still have the power to change, improve, and even save lives. Consider ways to turn up the volume on the words of encouragement you share with someone in your life—you never know when those words will become the Priceless Gift that changes a life forever!

19

You Are Never Too Old...
To Be Bold!

Please take notice: You are never too old to set another goal or to dream a new dream. An older gentleman approached me after I gave a speech a couple of years ago. He said, "You know, that was a great motivational speech for the young guys, but I've done all my work. There's nothing else for me to do now." He did not realize that from Moses to Grandma Moses, many amazing success stories begin late in life. If you're still on this planet, your business is NOT yet done.

At age 65, when most people are content to retire, a retiree named Colonel Harlan Sanders began to chase his dream. Armed with only a chicken recipe and a meager Social Security check, he set off to sell his recipe idea to restaurant owners in the hopes of making it big. Now that's not exactly a Harvard Business School-approved business plan.

He drove around the country, sleeping in his car, trying to find someone to back him. He kept changing his approach and knocking on doors. He was rejected 1,009 times, and then someone said "Yes." The colonel was in business. Despite being a chunky old man in a white suit, Colonel Sanders made a fortune because he was BOLD enough to pursue a seemingly unreasonable dream.

Another example is the late Sam Walton, son of a small-town Oklahoma banker. In 1945, he and his brother took out a $25,000 loan to open a five-and-dime that eventually grew into a chain of 15 Ben Franklin franchises. When the top executives at Ben Franklin refused to go along with Walton's idea of building bigger stores with smaller profit margins in small towns around the country, he set off on his own. Mr. Walton was 45 years old before he opened his first Wal-Mart store.

Most businessmen of that age would have played it safe. Sam Walton followed his own dream and became the most successful merchant of his time and, at one point, the nation's wealthiest man. When he died in 1992 at age 74, his company had 1,735 stores. His family fortune at that time was estimated to be in excess of $23 billion. Sam was also BOLD in the pursuit of his dream. And he achieved it.

It doesn't matter if you're 18 or 80—if you're still here on the planet, your business is not done. You still have a lot to give. Be bold, be bodacious...be BOLDACIOUS—so you can live your dreams and inspire others to live theirs TOO!

20

Find Your Own Spiritual Road

Just after sunrise, I hear the soothing sounds of my footsteps plodding along on the pavement below me, my labored breath, and the rippling flow of a nearby stream. I'm climbing the hill road on an early morning run through the woods of Trout Valley.

For over 25 years, several times a week, I have escaped pressure, distraction, worry, or fear by running. On the road, I seek my own mountain, my own desert, my own little island. I am away from the world, in nature, in peace, and in a silence that allows me to be me. I feel free.

I run along the river and over the hills, and I become one with my body. I delight in my energy, my strength, and my power as I take in the tall trees, the green fields, and the rushing water. In those moments I am a total and perfect runner—despite the fact I will never run a four-minute mile. I feel completely alive.

Running has become a form of meditation for me, a spiritual practice. I regularly experience what Georges Bernanos called the miracle of solitude and escape. He said, "The man who has not seen the road in the early light of morning, cool and living between two rows of trees, does not know hope." Bernanos even believed that man must possess himself in solitude and silence before he can be of real use to society.

Moments of solitude—being alone, reflecting, meditating, simply enjoying the sounds of silence—are necessary to find spiritual contentment. During the last few years of speaking around the country, I have had the privilege to meet some very extraordinary people. I can't think of a single person whom I have met that is inwardly peaceful who doesn't carve out a little time daily for some sort of spiritual practice.

Whether it be meditation, yoga, a 45-minute run in nature, or even a 10-minute soak in a hot bathtub, time spent quietly in spiritual reflection is critical for a vital life. Everyday trials are placed in better perspective and become more manageable.

As I finish the loop through Trout Valley woods and head for home, I have a new vision of myself and of the universe. The running is easy now, but full of power. I finish the run not knowing all the answers to my deep spiritual questions, but knowing that answers exist. And tomorrow, I will be back out on my spiritual road, searching for them one more time.

PART II

SALES

MOVES

20 Quick Tips to Improve Your Position in Business

21

Fall in Love with "No"

How many "no's" can you take? How many times have you wanted to go up and introduce yourself to an attractive person, or a potential client at a networking function, then decided not to because you didn't want to hear the word "no"? Have you ever decided not to try for a new job, make another sales call, or audition for a part because you didn't want to be rejected?

In sales, often the major difference between earning $250,000 per year and $60,000 per year is learning how to handle rejection, learning how to love "no," so that the fear of this word no longer stops us from taking action. The very best salespeople are the ones who are rejected the most. They take "no" as just a little prod to keep going till they hear "yes." Consciously or subconsciously, they are in love with "no." They have learned to give it a little internal hug by teaching themselves that it means they're just one step closer to "yes."

Think about the movie character Rocky, or the one called Rambo. Think about that guy Sylvester Stallone. Did he just show up one day at the studio and hear, "Hey, we like your body and your nice accent—we would like to put you in the movies"? Not exactly. Stallone became a success because he fell in love with "no." He was able to withstand rejection after rejection. He was rejected over 1,000 times when he first started out. But he kept pushing, kept trying, kept hugging those "no's," and finally ended up making a movie called *Rocky*. He was able to hear "no" 1,000 times and then still go on to knock on door number 1,001!

There are no real successes without rejection. The more rejection you get, the better you are, the more you have learned, the closer you are to your successful outcome. The next time some-body rejects you, give him or her a hug. They may look at you strangely, but it sure will be fun! Turn those "no's" into hugs. If you fall in love with "no," you'll be able to handle massive rejection, and by handling massive rejection, you'll eventually reach your goals.

22.

The Real Pros Still Prospect

Some salespeople think that prospecting and contacting new people to set up appointments are things you outgrow once you're a "veteran" and enjoying some steady business. You NEVER become experienced enough to ignore the fundamentals. The fundamentals form the foundation of success in any profession—especially selling!

Prospecting is the primary fundamental of the professional salesperson. Prospecting work drives the entire sales cycle. It leads to appointments that lead to interviews. Interviews then lead to qualified prospects, which eventually lead to sales.

The "real pros" never stray from practicing the fundamentals of their profession. Walter Cronkite, the most respected newsman of his era, was visiting a fellow TV newsman at his studio waiting to take him to dinner. While he was there, he found himself being stared at by all the younger reporters working at that particular station. Suddenly, there was the sound of a siren outside the office—a fire truck racing to a local fire. A junior reporter asked his boss if someone should go outside to cover the story. His boss replied "Son, we're a big-time news operation here! Didn't you see Mr. Cronkite in here? He has covered Vietnam, Watergate, the space program, and many other huge national stories. We are not going to look bad in front of him by responding to something as routine as a local fire."

And then, through the window, the cub reporter's boss saw something he would never forget. He saw America's #1 newsman dashing as fast as he could down the street to cover a breaking news story: a local fire. He realized then what Walter Cronkite already knew—the pros NEVER ignore the fundamentals.

By the same token, talking to new people is a critical part of a salesperson's job, and it's something you NEVER outgrow. So keep prospecting like the pro you are!

23.

Don't Forget Your SELL Phone

A lexander Graham Bell's invention maybe the greatest tool salespeople have ever known. Yet many salespeople who love to talk dread using the phone—it feels like a 100-pound weight in their hands. Using the telephone is definitely the most cost-effective way to reach customers or prospects. The telephone is also the most time-effective way to follow up with customers and stay in touch. Salespeople can become more effective by embracing the phone and realizing this modern convenience can truly have them Dialing for Dollars!

The key to maximizing the phone is to adhere to the following tips:

- Do your homework before the call. Be prepared!
- Call for a purpose. What do you want to accomplish?
- Have a positive attitude!
- Use a script if cold-calling.
- Keep the opening presentation close to 30 seconds.
- Leave voice mail no more than once per week.
- Carefully listen to their needs and wants.
- Use time to build the relationship.
- Paint pictures over the phone to better sell them.
- Document and track all calls, contacts, appointments, etc.
- Incorporate and schedule regular calling in your week.

Remember, the phone is an efficient tool, but just a tool. For most salespeople, it is not a substitute for personal contact with customers. If you recognize that the phone does not really weigh 100 pounds and follow the above tips, you'll be dialing for dollars with your NEW SELL PHONE!

24.

Sell to the "C" Level

If you want to win the BIG orders, you have to sell the decision-makers. And if you're selling big solutions for big money, these decision-makers are high-level executives. CEOs, CIOs, CFOs, COOs, Presidents, VPs, and other high-level decision-makers are known as the "C" level.

A plane must take off from the runway if it's going to climb high and reach the favorable jet stream winds. The salesperson wanting to make the big bucks must also leave the runway environment where all the low-level influencers reside and start climbing to an altitude where the executives are. They must climb higher to sell at the "C" level. The economic buyer or decision-maker is almost always at this level.

The salespeople most successful selling these "C" level executives are other executives. You may have experienced this yourself: Near the end of a big deal, your boss or another executive in your company comes in and closes the deal you spent months working on. You're a little angry! You did most of the work, and now your boss is taking an ego trip at your expense.

So how can you convince the top exec that you have the right stuff? You can start by acting like an executive, especially by trying to see things from the top down. Seeing things from 40,000 feet, the big picture, and being able to communicate that vision will go a long way to establishing rapport. By speaking this language of the "C" level, you'll be better able to persuade them.

Connecting with executives in their own specific language will win them over. John F. Kennedy was famous for this in his public addresses. During one of his speeches, he established incredible rapport with the German people, when he said, "Ich bin ein Berliner" during the Berlin Wall crisis. The crowd went wild! Speaking the exact language of the listener is a big key to rapport and very necessary in selling high-level executives.

The other key is your ability to command respect. In the business world, that respect comes from a number of behaviors and traits. Here's how you can build your executive demeanor:

1. Read several books on executive-level topics and thought processes.

2. Join a trade association for the industry you're selling to.

3. Read the executive-focused magazines and newspapers such as *Forbes, Fortune, Business Week, The Wall Street Journal*, etc.

4. Seek an executive mentor within your own organization whom you do not report to for development.

5. Listen and observe closely all the executives you get a chance to, in your organization and others.

6. Emulate their skills—listening, questioning, decision-making, communication, and business acumen.

7. Be sure you look the part and carry yourself as an executive. The quality of clothing they wear, what they drive, even down to what they take notes with, should be part of your demeanor as well.

One of the keys to making serious cash in sales is being able to sell to high-level executives. Leaving the comfort zone of the runway and climbing to sell at the "C" level will have your career flying to the next level. Donald Trump says, "I like thinking big. If you're going to be thinking anything, you might as well think big." So, if you're going to be selling to somebody, you might as well be selling to the BIG guys!

25.

Listen Up or Lose the Business

The salesperson thought he was listening when the prospect said she wanted to do a "big" sales training program. After the meeting, the salesperson put together an "awesome" proposal for a two-week, $35,000 sales training course and forwarded it to the client. After not hearing anything for several weeks, the salesperson called the prospect and was shocked to find out she thought the price of the proposal was "outrageous."

What happened? The salesperson was not listening closely when the prospect had shared that last year's training budget totaled only $5,000. If he had realized how small the company's budget was, he could have recommended a much smaller, less expensive program that the prospect would have received enthusiastically.

The importance of listening cannot be over-exaggerated in sales. And, although it is by far the single most important communications tool for salespeople, it's often overlooked in the majority of sales training programs today. Virtually no schools offer course work on listening, despite the fact that it is a learnable skill. Joey Asher, a trainer from Atlanta, teaches listening using the four-step FACE technique:

F - Focus on the person speaking. Pay attention.

A - Acknowledge the person speaking. Do not sit there like a lump. Let them know you are listening.

C - Clarify. Make sure you understand what is being said. Repeat back to the person speaking what they said.

E - Empathize: This is the step beyond clarification. You let them know that not only is the message clear, but you understand their position and what is bothering them.

Asher recommends talking 25% of the time and listening 75% of the time. If you learn to listen better by getting some training or at least practicing the FACE listening technique, you really will be listening up and not losing the sale!

26

Selling Is Serving

Sales Superstars seem to know, consciously or subconsciously, that the word "sell" originates from the Scandinavian root "selzig," which literally means "serve." As my first mentor, Zig Ziglar, always said, "You can get everything in life you want, if you will just help enough other people get what *they* want." Losing sight of this core principle by focusing on their commission, quarterly sales quota, or closing a hot deal quickly prevents many salespeople from becoming elite selling stars.

Like a great dog serves its master, Sales Superstars serve their customers and prospects and go to extraordinary lengths to find favor with their clientele. Past any obstacle, the faithful canine has been known to rescue a senior, defend a child, or even save its master's life. Sales Superstars must also do whatever it takes to serve their customers so fervently that an almost unbreakable customer loyalty develops. They are completely devoted to satisfying the needs of those they serve. This focus on service becomes a powerful sales tool indeed, because satisfied buyers not only remain loyal, but also tell others of the way they were treated.

How would your customers describe your level of service? If you focus and perform like salespeople from the following two companies, you can count yourself among the very elite. Nordstrom department store's salespeople are told, for example, "Use your own best judgment in all situations to make the customer happy." Their salespeople are legendary for going far beyond the call of duty. They have even gone to a competitor's store to buy a product for a customer if their store was out of the item. Just like Macy's department store in the movie *Miracle on 34th Street*, Nordstrom develops customers who are amazed at their service and keep coming back for more.

Salespeople and customer service personnel from the Ritz-Carlton Hotel are taught, "If a customer complains to you, you own the problem and must resolve the problem—no matter whom you must involve to get the job done." Frank Bucaro, author of *Taking the High Road*, shares a funny story of when he arrived at a Ritz-Carlton and complained to the bellman of a very full bladder. Because of their policy for handling customer problems themselves, the bellman took Frank directly to the men's restroom himself. At the restroom door, Frank nervously asked, "You're not coming in, are you?" The bellman replied, "No! No! Our service definitely stops at the door!" Frank's story, though humorous, definitely illustrates how an extraordinary level of service is never forgotten by a customer.

Customers who have experienced super-service by a salesperson, or anybody else in a company, will definitely tell others about their experiences. Word of mouth will accelerate a salesperson's positive reputation, transforming it into their ultimate marketing tool. A fast-spreading reputation for high-level service will dramatically increase sales, and it's what often moves the average salesperson one click closer to becoming one of the world's Sales Superstars.

27.

Low-Tech Sales Tools Rule

Effective, efficient selling does not require lots of high-tech gadgetry. Stephan Schiffman, author of *High-Efficiency Selling,* points out that snazzy spread-sheets, complicated flip charts, or four-color brochures are not needed. If you have these tools, by all means use them, as long as they do not interfere with why you showed up in the first place—and that is to ask the right questions. One of the major keys to being a Sales Superstar is being an effective interviewer. Effective interviewing takes time—it should probably occupy 75% of the sales cycle. Effective interviewing finds a way to build around the question "What are you trying to accomplish here?" Sales Superstars will use the gold medal technique of letting the prospect tell them what to do. They will give up the need to maintain control, and they will utilize proper ASKING techniques. Sales Superstars give the prospect plenty of room to breathe before they begin making any recommendation on what they might have to offer—in short, they are very patient.

Because effective interviewing is at the heart of selling, several fundamental, distinctly low-tech tools are needed by the Sales Superstar. The following five low-tech tools make the interviewing phase more efficient and more effective no matter what else you bring to the call.

1. Your appearance

No matter how fancy your brochure or Palm Pilot, if your appearance is unprofessional, you will not be taken seriously. If your clothes, hair, or teeth are not well kept, you have an obstacle to overcome. The initial purpose of any interview is to get the prospect to open up to you, and good grooming is essential to that.

2. Your briefcase

Make a stylish, attractive briefcase your only accessory as you walk in the room for the first time. Just as with your appearance, you only get one chance for a first impression, and you do not want to blow it by walking in juggling boxes, samples, or other items.

3. A yellow legal pad and a nice pen

A yellow legal pad and a nice-looking pen are the most powerful tools a salesperson can use during the interviewing phase. When you take out the pad and encourage the prospect to talk, you communicate several important things:

- The prospect has the floor.
- He or she has your undivided attention.
- You are engaged in finding out what he or she does and what he or she needs.
- You are organized.
- You are trustworthy.
- The prospect is a big shot.

This low-tech tool will bring amazing results!

4. Your client list

Give the prospect a copy even if he or she does not ask for it. It shares the names of others you have helped.

5. Your calendar

The physical presence of your calendar communicates you are busy and that you are encouraging your prospect to commit to a date to continue the process.

The Sales Superstar never forgets that the low-tech tools RULE when interviewing prospects.

28

Use the Eight-Point Buyer Checklist

Top-quality research is vital for today's selling professional. You must do your homework on buyers to qualify them, to prioritize them as buyers, to better establish rapport with them, and to handle any preconceived objections they might have. The following acronym (BEND 4P's) can serve as a great guide to what information is critical to secure:

B - BELIEFS: What does the buyer believe about you, your product or service, your competitor, etc.?

E - EVALUATION PROCESS: How will the buyer evaluate your product? What criteria will he or she use?

N - NEEDS: What does the buyer really need?

D - DESIRES: What does the buyer really want?

P - PSYCHIC WOUNDS: Does the buyer have any ill will toward your company, you, or a particular type of product or service?

P - PERSONAL INTERESTS: What are the buyer's hobbies, his or her family life, favorite sports, etc.?

P - PERSONAL MENTORS: Whom does the buyer look to for similar buying decisions? What references will he or she accept?

P - PERSONAL SUCCESSES: What is the buyer proud of? What has he or she purchased before that gave him or her a personal win?

Remember to get answers to the BEND 4P QUESTIONS, and you'll be better armed to better serve the buyer and Close the Sale!

29.

Compliments Are Weapons of Influence

Great salespeople must learn every tool to more effectively influence their prospects. Improved skills will lead to being able to better meet the needs of those they call on. There are a number of tools—or Weapons of Influence, as Robert Cialdini, Ph.D. calls them—which we can all use to help persuade people to see the benefits of our service or product. If we use these weapons with integrity, rather than as an attempt to manipulate our prospects, they will help us break down the barriers that many people naturally put up in any selling situation.

Actor McLean Stevenson once described how his wife tricked him into marriage: "She said she liked me." Although designed for a laugh, the comment is more instructive than most of us realize. When someone pays us a compliment, it can have an almost hypnotic effect for producing a liking response and then a willing compliance. Joe Girard, the world's "greatest car salesperson," has always said the key to his success was getting customers to like him. He did something that, on the face of it, seems foolish and costly. Every month he sent every one of his more than 13,000 former customers and prospects a card with a seasonal message on the cover but the same message inside. He never varied the inside message—it simply read "I Like You." As Joe explained it, "There is nothing else on the card. Just my name and me telling 'em that I like 'em."

Every month the message "I Like You" came from Joe like clockwork. Could a statement of liking so impersonal, so obviously designed to sell cars, really work? Joe thinks so, and his track record in sales warrants our considering his input. Research also supports his ideas. In an experiment done on men in North Carolina, researchers showed that we are very influenced by compliments and praise. Three groups of men received comments from someone who needed a favor. One group got compliments only. The second group got compliments and some negative comments, and the third group got only negative comments.

There were three findings. First, the person providing only compliments was liked best by the men. Second, this was true even though the men realized the person providing the compliments stood to gain from being liked by them. And third, the praise did not even have to be accurate to work. As salespeople, we must realize that people have such a strong and positive response to flattery that this is a Weapon of Influence we must utilize. It will help our prospects lower their barriers and ultimately make them more receptive to being helped by our services or products. While we might not want to send 150,000 compliment cards a year, sharing a little praise during our sales calls can definitely make a difference.

Dress to Sell

With the advent of ventures such as "dot-coms" and "casual Fridays," there is often confusion in the marketplace as to how salespeople ought to dress. While in-house dress codes may have relaxed, you cannot afford to dress cheaply when you're selling to businesspeople and higher income customers. You will look and feel more powerful when you're well dressed. In fact, the best rule for buying clothing is to pay *twice* as much money and get *half* as many clothes. It is better that you pay *more* than you feel you can afford but that you buy *fewer* articles. Buy good-quality clothing in natural fabrics such as wool or cotton and be DRESSED TO SELL!

Get Physical: Involve the Prospect for a More Effective Presentation

"Lena, just press that green button to open the chamber door," was all I said. The group from Chicago stepped in closer and watched with amazement as the door opened. Then I handed a new high-tech cassette for dispensing sterilant to another prospect and said, "Woody, just insert it here, and the machine will pull it in the rest of the way." Again the group let out some 'oohs' and 'aahs' after Woody had inserted the cassette. Next I said, "Diana, please put those trays in the chamber." Diana slid two bright blue trays into the deep chamber and commented, "This chamber holds much more than I thought it could." The group nodded in agreement, and I continued my sales presentation.

The presentation described above took place in 1994 in the sterilization area at Long Beach Memorial Hospital, in Long Beach, California. I was with a group of prospects from Chicago who had flown out to see a brand new low-temperature sterilization technology called Plasma Sterilization. That day, quite by accident, I discovered a very powerful selling technique that led to many more sales in the years that followed.

When we are demonstrating the capabilities of our products in a sales presentation, the more physical involvement we can get by the prospects during the process, the more we can lead them toward a feeling of ownership. Tactile involvement used early and often during the entire sales process engages more of our prospects' senses, which in turn creates greater emotional involvement.

Emotional involvement can generate greater sales. Customer *motion* leads straight to customer *emotion* and vice versa. Physical involvement also helps us find out how receptive prospects are by watching their non-verbal actions. Most prospects are not skilled actors, so when we involve them physically, we can gauge where they are in terms of moving from resistance toward acceptance of what we're offering.

Usually it is easier to get a prospect involved in a product sale than in a service sale. But if we use our creativity, we will be amazed at the ways in which we can involve a prospect. Below are some ideas to consider.

INVOLVEMENT IN THE PRESENTATION SETUP

1. Ask for help with an easel, projector, or video machine.
2. Ask for something—a pencil, paper, Magic Marker.
3. Ask them to plug something in or move something.
4. Accept the offered coffee or soda.
5. Use the setup time for humor and small talk too.

INVOLVEMENT IN THE PRODUCT DEMONSTRATION

1. Get them to run the demo.
2. Get them to push the buttons.
3. Get them to work the copier, drive the car, walk the property.
4. Get them to hold something.
5. Get them to help you assemble something.
6. Get them to actually use the product and experience the benefits.

Even though we know how to do it, we are not going to impress the prospect much with a whiz-bang demonstration. All we're going to do is bore them if we don't get them physically involved.

We must try to get the prospect to lead the entire presentation if possible. The more involved we get them, the more ownership they experience, and the closer we move to an affirmative decision.

The group members all loaded the Plasma Sterilizer with wrapped surgical instruments, and we left for lunch. We returned an hour later, and the prospects were shocked to find the sterilization cycle completed. The process they all had been using back in their Chicago hospitals often required as long as 18 hours to deliver sterile instrumentation. "Go ahead, open the door, unload her, and examine YOUR load," I said to the group.

Those eight sterilization professionals excitedly pushed the buttons, opened the door, unwrapped the load, and then acted almost like kids at Christmas operating a new toy. They had all moved a giant step closer to purchasing the new technology. In fact, seven of the eight prospects did eventually purchase Low-Temperature Plasma Sterilizers, which represented more than a half million dollars in sales revenue.

What I learned that day is to always get more of the sales prospects' senses involved. I learned you have to follow the title of the popular song by Olivia Newton-John, "Let's Get Physical!" if you want to generate more sales.

32.

Ask for Some Extra Business

Here's an amazing statistic: After giving a complete presentation about the benefits of their product or service, more than 60% of salespeople and businesspeople never ask for the order. Over half of the folks who need you to buy their product don't actually come out and ask you to buy it. If you want to improve sales success or business growth, you've got to ask prospects to buy what you're selling!

Use your kids as role models in how to ask for more business this year. They are the masters! Their formula is to ask until they get what they want. If you've ever taken a child into a grocery or toy store, then you've witnessed how easily and often they ask for the sale. Obtaining your commitment to buy something for them comes quite naturally. It is only as adults that we seem to have lost our ability to ask for business.

At the fifth hole at the Elks Country Club and golf course in Fort Wayne, Indiana, an eight-year-old named Timmy beautifully demonstrated how to ask for business. As our foursome reached the fifth hole tee area on a hot, sunny July day, there was the usual back-up of golfers—because it was a par three hole. Near the tee box was a small wooden table with two big, plastic jugs and a stack of glasses. One jug was filled with lemonade and the other with iced tea. Timmy smiled broadly and yelled to our foursome, "Would you like a cool drink while you're waiting?" We all walked over to the fence, still not saying anything yet. Timmy asked again, "Do you want some lemonade or do you prefer iced tea?" Timmy made four sales, collected the money, and then told us to "Have a nice day!"

How often do you think Timmy asks for business? You're right if you guessed every single time someone shows up at the fifth hole tee. Timmy had no 10-week sales training course. He sold naturally! Like Timmy, you must always ask a closing question to secure the business. Don't waffle, or talk around it, or even worse, wait for your prospect to ask you.

Simply ask for the sale. "Would you like to give it a try?" is an example that works well. "Where are we going to ship this?" is another good way to move things forward. There are a multitude of ways to ask for the business, and developing a dozen or so appropriate for your product or service is a surefire strategy to increase business.

Furthermore, when most sales and business people do ask for business, they rarely try to sell additional products or services after they have secured the first sale. Most salespeople are so delighted to get the sale, they forget to try to make additional sales when the prospect is still in their presence.

The key is to always be thinking of other complementary products or services you could sell them right when you have them. This is often called a "cross-sell" or "upsell." In the car industry, once you've purchased a vehicle, you'll probably be asked to buy an extended warranty for a few hundred dollars more, or rust-proofing to protect the car's finish.

What else could you be asking for when you do business? One more question at the end of the sale could significantly increase your income. Many years ago, McDonald's came up with a unique way to ask for extra business. They trained their staff to ask one more question when someone ordered a hamburger and a drink. That single question added more than $20 million to their bottom line. The question was, "Would you like fries with that?" Obviously, a lot of people responded with, "Sure, why not." Here's what's worth noting: How often do they ask that question? Every single time!

Remember to ask for the business and some extra business—just like the kids and McDonald's always do. You will be surprised by the affirmative answers you get!

33.

Unlock the Gatekeeper to Get More Business

Gatekeepers often seem like the "enemy," as we try to get past them to reach the decision-makers, whom we know will benefit from our products or services. We may even feel like getting through the receptionist is just one big headache! From my sales training course, *Cracking the Code: Super Powers of the Sales Stars*, there are a couple of quick tips that will help you remove the barriers and unlock the gatekeeper to get more business:

1. Be relentlessly upbeat!

2. Politely confirm that the person you're trying to reach handles the areas you want to discuss.

3. Use a "resource proclamation" that outlines what you're offering the customer in a simple and succinct manner.

4. Develop a response to the inevitable "What is this regarding?"—one that will encourage decision-makers to either take the call or call you back.

5. Deliver your message in a confident, but not too aggressive, tone of voice. The idea is to come across as powerful— not overbearing, intimidating, or shady. You want to be charming, optimistic, and authoritative.

Your tone of voice plays an immensely important role in getting through to the people you want to reach. Practice your pitch in a tape recorder until it sounds natural and compelling. Follow these tips so you can remove the barriers and "Unlock the Gatekeeper to Get More Business."

34

Remember PAPA for Your First Client Meeting

When you're meeting a prospect for the first time, you should start with the social conventions and "icebreaker" dialog to warm things up and help build rapport. Questions and dialog can be about the office setting, hobbies, mutual contacts, or anything that can begin building the bridge between you and the prospect. This is also your time to match and mirror the prospect's physiology without being manipulative. Sales Superstars do this unconsciously, while others must learn these valuable skills. When the trust and comfort are up, you can bridge to the real meeting. I developed a simple acronym to keep you on track for first interviews with prospective clients. Just remember your PAPA— see his picture in your mind!

P - Present a very brief, benefit-laden commercial about your company and products.

A - Ask about the prospect's past, present, and future experience in the key areas.

P - Present a recommendation that begins, "Based on what I've heard today…"

A - Ask for an agreement to set up a second appointment.

So remember, your PAPA is the key to getting from the first sales interview to the second!

35.

Use the Art of the Flinch in Negotiating

Great sales negotiators know you should always *flinch*—which means react with shock and surprise at a buyer's proposal or counter proposal. When you're in a clothing store and you ask the clerk, "How much is that suit?" and they respond "$1,500"—you cannot respond with "That's not bad!" You must act as if you are having a heart attack when you hear the price!

Perhaps you're thinking that it is beneath your dignity to flinch, but the truth of the matter is that when buyers, or sellers, make a proposal or a counter proposal, they're watching for the reaction. They may not think that you as a salesperson will agree, but they have thrown it out to see what your reaction will be. For example:

- You sell medical equipment and the buyer asks you to include an extended warranty.
- You sell yellow page advertising and the buyer wants you to throw in a second ad at no charge.
- You sell cars and the buyer wants you to throw in rust-proofing.

In each of these situations the buyer probably thought you would not go along with it, but if you don't flinch and act surprised, they'll automatically think they can get you to go along with it. It triggers them to want to be "The Tough Negotiator" and see how far you'll go.

Flinching is critical because most people believe more what they see than what they hear. The visual overrides the auditory for most people. Do not dismiss flinching as childish or too theatrical until you've had a chance to see how effective it can really be. When I flinched at the price of the suit in the clothing store, they reduced the price by $600 to $900 immediately! A woman I taught the technique to said she has had her bottle of wine discounted several times at fine restaurants. If you have not added flinching to your selling skills, you'll be surprised when you first see how effective it is. The Art of the Flinch will have you selling at higher profit margins and may even get you a better deal on your next bottle of wine or clothing purchase.

36

Roller Coaster Rides:
Great for Fun, Bad for Sales

At Cedar Point, an amusement park in Sandusky, Ohio, I was screaming with joy, hanging on for dear life, as we plunged several hundred feet toward the finish of the Blue Streak Roller Coaster. What an awesome rush of speed and adrenaline. I fell in love with roller coasters that day in 1967. They were—and still are—great fun for me.

Many years later, in 1985, I went on a different type of roller coaster ride. Early in my sales career, selling defibrillators for a division of Eli Lilly, I enjoyed a huge first quarter followed by a second quarter slump. This was my first exposure to THE ROLLER COASTER EFFECT, often experienced in sales. Unlike the roller coaster in Sandusky, this ride is no fun for anyone. It amounts to big commissions one quarter, followed by eating at fast food joints the next. Sales managers hate THE ROLLER COASTER EFFECT too, because their forecasts become suspect in the eyes of senior management. Manufacturing execs, with just-in-time inventories, also pull their hair out because they never know how much to produce. Let's face it—when it comes to sales, a roller coaster ride is no fun at all.

I later learned that THE ROLLER COASTER EFFECT in sales comes from letting the sales funnel run dry. A dry funnel leads to sales dips that, in turn, leave salespeople hanging on for dear life. Nine out of ten salespeople, when they finally do discover their funnels are empty, will prospect like crazy to refill them. But there is always a lag for their efforts which creates the very up and down effect I've been describing. Very few salespeople ever have two great back-to-back selling quarters because they prospect out of panic one quarter, and then close their few best prospects the next.

The solution for reducing, and eventually eliminating, THE ROLLER COASTER EFFECT is in how we arrange our work priorities. The key is to allocate your time based around this priority:

1. **Always close your best few!**
    These are the prospects that are so close to closing that to neglect them hands them directly to the competition. This activity also guarantees a regular commission stream.

2. **Prospect, qualify, and fill the funnel.**
    This is what we usually put off until we're at the crisis stage. Filling the funnel with new leads every week, every month, and every quarter goes a long way toward smoothing out the roller coaster track.

3. **Work the rest of your leads through the funnel, toward the bottom, for closure.**
    Most salespeople spend too much time here, instead of making sure new leads are entering their funnels. While important, these activities should never be at the expense of closing your best few, or filling the funnel with new leads.

If we follow these priorities, we can still enjoy the experience of a wild roller coaster ride, but it will be at the amusement park and not in our sales results. And while I have to admit that I have still had my ups and downs in sales since 1985, I can also tell you that my commitment to never letting the funnel run dry has made the track considerably smoother for me.

37.

Put Your Overalls On: Good Selling Is Like Good Farming

If you're a farmer and you want a good crop in August, what must you do? One thing I learned growing up in Indiana was that farmers plan months ahead: soil improvement, tilling, and seeding are all done in the spring. The farmer does the bulk of the work on the front end. He manages, nurtures, and tends on the front end and then waits for everything to grow to harvest.

For salespeople, the sales cycle is the growing season. If the salesperson can plant enough seeds, nurture and tend those seeds, and plan for possible damage, he or she can harvest the crop at the end of the growing season without cramming. Cramming has never worked on the farm, and it produces poor results in sales as well. Like good farmers, Sales Superstars plant in advance, but unlike farmers, they must keep planting new crops every month to keep a continual harvest all year-round.

Sales Superstars focus on two things if they want to use the farm as their model: (1) the number of qualified prospects in the sales funnel and (2) their status in the funnel. How many have you got, how would you grade them, and what are the chances that you can close each prospect?

If the number of qualified prospects is low, they must plant some more seeds—find new prospects to fill the funnel. If grading their prospects in the sales funnel reveals one or more that are shaky, then a plan must be developed to strengthen the situation and move those prospects closer to obtaining a commitment. Just as the farmer must eliminate the weeds, the Sales Superstar must eliminate any factors that slow the harvesting of business in her sales funnel.

Sales executives and managers often forget to behave like farmers too. Because American corporations have a prevalent short-term focus on what needs to be harvested this month, many managers and executives deceive themselves (usually unintentionally) about their sales prospects, sales funnels, and sales forecasts.

Let's face it—salespeople hate to do forecasts, and so when they see their manager coming, they give them the old "hot-air pump" forecast. The "hot-air pump" forecast is all inflated with nothing but HOT prospects—those that have a "90% chance" of closing. This is the way salespeople keep their managers off their backs for another 30 days. These forecasts are rarely close to accurate.

Sales managers then massage the forecast and change it by some percentage factor they developed, and then they turn it over to senior management. Usually, by the time it reaches the top levels, it is so far off that it has been a huge waste of time and resources. It also creates a lot of unnecessary stress.

So how can sales managers and senior executives behave more like farmers and get better sales results? They must plan longer term, remembering that more emphasis is always needed on sowing than on reaping. A few changes are necessary for this implementation:

- First-line managers must shift from pressuring their people about closing business this month to helping them build a quality funnel.

- Senior management must shift from pressuring field managers to close business this month to encouraging them to build and accurately report quality funnel activity.

- Compensation should be in place to motivate managers to manage the process.

- The funnel must be graded consistently and accurately across the entire sales organization.

- Senior management must review the funnel on a regular basis and conduct quality assurance.

Honest prospect and funnel appraisal by salespeople, sales managers, and top executives results in proactive selling, greater sales, and a lot less anxiety. Salespeople, sales managers, and senior executives will all gain a competitive edge if they'll put their "overalls" on and begin to approach selling the same way farmers approach planting.

38

Learn the Tricks of the Trade Show

I t's time for your annual trade show, business fair, or convention. Hundreds of your customers, prospects, suppliers, and competitors will be in the same town for two to five days. Nowhere else can you see such a concentration of people in your industry. What an opportunity! Selling, prospecting, and relationship-building possibilities are gargantuan—you have no time to waste!

It's all about time, and the proper use of it. If 4,000 people will attend during the three-day, 30-hour span, what should you do? What strategies and tactics should you follow? How will you maximize your time? Many people go to conventions to just get away, or have a good time. This cannot be your primary objective! You need to be at 100% of your game from the minute you get on the plane until you wearily make your way back home from the airport.

Here are some "tricks of the trade show" to have up your sleeve that will maximize your effectiveness and sales results. These 18 points will put more money in your pocket. You do want to make more money, don't you?

1. Be prepared. Have your presentation material ready and rehearsed before you depart.

2. Develop your game plan before you leave your office or home. Have a strategy for the show.

3. Stay in the main/best hotel. For a few extra dollars the payoff is big.

4. Get there a day early. You'll be more relaxed and ready.

5. Target 10 customers. Build your key relationships.

6. Target 10 prospects. Connect. Build rapport.

7. Be the first to arrive and the last to leave every day. It gives you an edge.

8. Read badges quickly. Stay alert for your people.

9. Be brief and to the point. Have a strong 60-second opener.

10. Diagnose buyer need and obtain information before you prescribe or sell anything.

11. Show how you solve problems. Focus on serving.

12. Get their contact info. This is critical!

13. Close for a next step with hot leads. Don't drop the ball.

14. Have fun and be funny. Enthusiasm and humor are contagious.

15. Regroup at night and plan for the next day.

16. Limit your alcohol—this isn't the time to make a fool of yourself.

17. Get the list of all show attendees.

18. Have a great time! Don't press or appear pressured— it will show.

If you employ these "tricks of the trade show"—you will capitalize on the best sales contact opportunity and the most fun time a salesperson can have in growing his or her business.

39

Leave 'em with a Little Lagniappe

I was traveling back from giving a motivational speech for a group of local business people when my Audi sputtered to a stop. I could not believe my brand new car would not run or start. Angry, I called Audi to chew them out. They immediately apologized and said they would have a flatbed truck to tow me within the hour. They showed up 45 minutes later with the tow, and I accompanied them to the dealership. That was the fastest I had ever gotten a tow.

As I walked in, still fuming despite the fast tow, they quickly approached me and said they had a brand new Jeep Cherokee waiting as a loaner until my Audi was fixed. They said I could leave immediately, and again they apologized for the breakdown. They also emphasized there would be no cost for anything!

I was beginning to cool down and was just leaving the building when the service manager offered to pay for my lunch at the restaurant of my choice. He wanted to compensate me for the inconvenience my car's breakdown had caused. As I was eating, I remembered the old sales and customer service technique of leaving your customer with a little lagniappe. The Audi dealership had left me with a little lagniappe.

Lagniappe (lan-yap) is a French word for "a little something extra or an unexpected gift." Many years ago in New Orleans, French store owners used lagniappe as a reward to attract and keep their customers. They had discovered a key strategy for maintaining customer loyalty.

For example, if a customer ordered five pounds of sugar, the clerk would dish out five pounds on the scale and then, with a smile, add an additional measure and say "lagniappe." That was the store owner's way of adding a little extra value and saying that your business was important.

My point is simply this: Customers enjoy positive surprises, especially when they're having problems with your product. Whether you're a salesperson or business owner, you must not forget to provide positive experiences for your customers. Customers enjoy getting a little something extra that is over and above their expectations. Leaving 'em with a little lagniappe is a great way to do this. Get creative with the lagniappe—it doesn't have to be clever, expensive, or time-consuming. Just add a little something extra.

On top of getting my free meal, Audi followed up by phone two weeks later to inquire if I was happy with the service I received. Would I ever buy another Audi, or recommend the brand to someone else? I just did!

40.

How to Make More Sales with Less Effort

The most valuable skill for reducing your sales effort is to learn how to market yourself effectively so that you barely have to sell at all. Personal Marketing is the fastest way to sell more and work less. It is simply getting your prospects excited about you and your service before you ever make a sales call. This is a concept that will open your eyes and change your life. If you follow a few tricks of the trade, you'll soon discover how simple it is to increase sales while reducing your selling effort.

Personal Marketing is the strategy of rarely speaking to anyone who does not already know who you are. It is applying advance marketing techniques before you meet a prospect. Here's a simple formula to show you how it works:

$$SE \times PM = SR$$

(Selling Effort x Personal Marketing = $ales Results)

It's simple math: The more marketing you do, the less Selling Effort you have to put forth. Selling Effort is physical, time-consuming, and fraught with objections and rejections. It requires great time management and communication skills. Personal Marketing is leveraging your message to as many of your target prospects as possible without your physically having to do it yourself. Develop and execute a few of the Personal Marketing strategies suggested below, and sales will come to you, rather than you chasing them.

Developing a referral stream through marketing efforts will greatly accelerate your sales. Good Personal Marketing—such as ads or links on web sites, a well-placed headline in a trade journal, or a best-selling book that refers to your services—will sell more than you ever could by just knocking on doors. By using media that reach thousands, you are in essence knocking on the door of everyone who sees them.

Keep in mind this is completely separate from the global marketing your company is already doing for you. This is a much more personalized and direct marketing effort that will not only draw prospects to your product or service, but direct them to you. Be sure the message you use is compelling enough to get them to act or show interest in what you have to offer.

Here are a few strategies to get you started. There are many more possible.

1. Create alliances with other individuals or companies who are in touch with your prospects.
2. Mail out sales letters.
3. Speak at local trade shows or bring a speaker in to an event you organized.
4. Advertise.
5. Join and participate in your trade associations.
6. Do e-mail or direct-mail marketing.
7. Ask for referrals and testimonials.
8. Volunteer at community events.
9. Attend networking functions.
10. Write an article for your industry and submit it to your trade publications.

These are only a few ways to market yourself as a salesperson to increase your sales results.

The problem is most salespeople do not want to spend the time or money necessary for marketing. They would rather be cheap and rely on their own physical effort or hope the company does the marketing for them. Those salespeople who rely only on their own sales effort will always have to work harder than those who market themselves personally.

So, if you want to sell more with less effort—give Personal Marketing a try. And if you do, please give me a call on your cell phone from the sunny tropical location where you'll be vacationing to celebrate all your sales success!

PART III

LIFE-CHANGING QUOTES

20 Quick Tips from the Wise

Oprah Winfrey

"The best thing about getting older is that you can really begin to think about your calling, your passion... When I look into the future, it is so bright, it burns my eyes."

—Oprah Winfrey

Have you ever wondered what your calling was? As Deepak Chopra points out, "A life of purpose is the purpose of life." Don't most of us go after things backwards? Instead of being blinded by our future, we blindly seek jobs that will allow us to make money and obtain the status we think we need. And then we end up struggling for years, often decades, trying to find out what's *really* important in our life.

Instead of choosing our vocation and then trying to figure out what's important to us, we need to first reflect upon what our passions are and act upon them secondly. As Epictetus said nearly two thousand years ago, "Know first who you are. Then dress accordingly." We must throw off the confining cloak of "should do's" and "have to do's" and discover how we can serve ourselves and others by doing the things we love to do and are good at doing. We'll experience creative love and joy as we work at what really matters—our purpose. Life is too short to squander—we must find our calling so that our future will be so bright we have to wear sunglasses.

William James

"There is a law in psychology that if you form a picture in your mind of what you would like to be, and you keep and hold that picture there long enough, you will soon become exactly as you had been thinking."

—William James (1842–1910)

William James was one of the strongest proponents for abandoning the philosophy of determinism, and is considered by many to be the father of American psychology. This idea of forming a picture in our minds is often referred to as visualization and is based on the Biblical notion "As you think, so shall you be." It goes far beyond positive thinking and holds the power to take our desires, goals, and dreams to a much higher level than we can ever imagine.

We think in pictures and we dream in pictures. Not in words or sentences, but in mental images. The words we use are only symbols to help us describe those pictures we see. William James states that we can control the picturing process. We are the director and producer of our pictures. If we create the picture we want for our lives, "hold on to that picture long enough," don't let anyone weaken it, we will develop that picture into reality. Our picture can become a box office smash hit that features us as the leading star!

Victor E. Frankl

*"The last of the human freedoms is to choose
one's attitude in any given set of circumstances."*
—Victor E. Frankl (1905–1997)

Internationally renowned psychiatrist Victor Frankl endured years of unspeakable horror in Nazi death camps. Because of his suffering, Dr. Frankl developed a revolutionary approach to psychotherapy known as logotherapy. One of the core principles of his theory is the belief that no matter what adversities we find ourselves confronted with, we can choose our attitude. He documents that people who chose to have a positive and resourceful attitude, even if they were suffering, experienced a richer, deeper meaning to life.

Through his experiences of suffering, Frankl discovered that people who have a strong enough purpose for pursuing a goal can endure any circumstance they're confronted with. Prisoners whose purpose for living centered around caring for loved ones or pursuing a life of significance were able to endure much more pain than those whose futures lacked hope. Greater awareness of our deepest core values and a more profound sense of life's meaning allow us to adopt a positive attitude more easily. That attitude will carry us through any challenge or struggle we ever face.

George Bernard Shaw

*"I want to be thoroughly used up when I die—for
the harder I work, the more I live. I rejoice in life
for its own sake. Life is no 'brief candle' to me; it is
a sort of splendid torch which I have got hold of for
the moment, and I want to make it burn as brightly
as possible before handing it on to future generations."*
—George Bernard Shaw (1856–1950)

Shaw, who lived into his nineties, wants us to remember that
every day is a splendid torch—a torch to brightly illuminate
our lives in a magnificent way. He reminds us not to take our
music to the grave with us! We must work hard, have new interests,
take on new projects, and become fully consumed by life. Then,
and only then, can we truly rejoice, knowing we have been
thoroughly used up. We have then poured all of our energy into
our own heroic mission, which becomes a torch to be passed on
to future generations.

Walking Buffalo

"Hills are always more beautiful than stone buildings, you know. Living in a city is an artificial existence. Lots of people hardly ever feel the soil under their feet, see plants grow except in flower pots, or get far enough beyond the street light to catch the enchantment of a night sky studded with stars. When people live far from scenes of the Great Spirit's making, it's easy for them to forget…"
—Walking Buffalo (1871–1967)

Walking Buffalo reminds us that the natural world, created by God, far exceeds anything man-made. This wise and famous Native American suggests that authentic existence is connected to living in, or at least being aware of, natural spaces. He points to the sacredness, enchantment, and beauty of Mother Earth. He is not recommending that we all leave our modern life and move to the wilderness, but he does highlight how easy it is to get disconnected from the harmony of nature when we exist in a modern urban environment. Taking time to experience the air, water, mountains, ocean, soil, rock, trees, clouds, animals, birds, and even insects will give us a new perspective on how we see our own lives. We must make the time to let our bodies, minds, and souls get into the rhythm of God's precious creation. When we walk barefoot on the earth and listen to all the natural sounds, we will reconnect to the sacred and reverent web of life.

46.

Michelangelo

*"The greatest danger for most of us is
not that our aim is too high and we miss
it, but that it is too low and we reach it"*
—Michelangelo (1475–1564)

Important dreams, big goals, high expectations—these are what Michelangelo Buonarroti tells us to reach for. Don't be seduced by the notion that there can be danger in aiming too high. In fact, it will be our hopes that will drive us to create masterpieces just like he did. We must make our own lives masterpieces! We are divinely created by God and thus come hardwired into that miraculous creating power. Let's keep hope alive by remembering what Albert Einstein said, "Great spirits have always encountered opposition from mediocre minds." So we must aim high, have hope, and not be swayed by the mediocre!

Ohiyesa

*"Friendship is held to be the severest test of character.
It is easy, we think, to be loyal to family and clan, whose
blood is in our veins. Love between a man and a woman
is founded on the mating instinct and is not free from
desire and self-seeking. But to have a friend, and to be
true under any and all trials, is the mark of a man!"*

—Ohiyesa (Santee Sioux)

Thomas Jefferson, my boyhood hero, met a man named James Madison in 1776 and worked with him to further the American Revolution and later shape a new government. From that work together sprang a friendship perhaps incomparable in intimacy, in trustfulness of collaboration, and in duration: it lasted 50 years. It was the embodiment of the kind of friendship Ohiyesa describes. These were friends who remained true under all their trials—men of virtue and character.

Four and a half months before he died—when he was ailing, debt-ridden, and worried about his impoverished family—Thomas Jefferson wrote to his life-long friend. His words, and Madison's reply, remind us that real friends are friends until death.

Jefferson wrote:

"The friendship which has subsisted between us now half a century and the harmony of our political principles and pursuits have been sources of constant happiness to me through that long period. It has also been a great solace to me to believe that you are engaged in vindicating to posterity the course we have pursued for preserving to them in all their purity the blessings of self-government which we had assisted in acquiring for them. If ever the earth has beheld a system of administration conducted with a single and steadfast eye to the general interest of happiness of those committed to it, one which protected by truth can never know reproach, it is that to which our lives have been devoted. To myself you have been a pillar of support through life. Take care of me when dead, and be assured that I shall leave you with my last affections."

A week later Madison replied:

"You cannot look back to the long period of our private friendship and political harmony with more affecting recollections than I do. If they are a source of pleasure to you, what ought they not to be to me? We cannot be deprived of the happy consciousness of the pure devotion to the public good with which we discharged the trust committed to us. And I indulge a confidence that sufficient evidence will find its way to another generation to insure, after we are gone, whatever of justice may be withheld whilst we are here."

In the best friendships, we see in perhaps its purest form a moral paradigm for all human relations. Like Ohiyesa poignantly described—the real mark of a man, or woman, is to be an enduring, authentic friend.

Gandhi

"Strength of numbers is the delight of the timid.
The Valiant in spirit glory in fighting alone."
—Gandhi (1869–1948)

Living out our most heartfelt dreams and creating a life of purpose—even trying to articulate what those dreams are—can be frightening. We often share our dreams with others in the hope that their support will provide us with the strength to take a new risk or seek a radical vision. Unfortunately, what often happens is that others respond by telling us to "get real."

We can find support, though, in the comments of Mahatma Gandhi. He suggests that seeking consensus to pursue a dream is "the delight of the timid." Perhaps there's a kind of sacred glory in reaching for goals that everyone else thinks are "crazy" or beyond our grasp. The endorsement of others may feel good at the moment, but our dreams may materialize with a sweeter success if we abandon our efforts to gain others' approval.

49.

Mother Theresa

*"There should be less talk; a preaching point is not
a meeting point. What do you do then? Take a broom
and clean someone's house. That says enough."*
—Mother Theresa (1910–1997)

Tiny Mother Theresa, the spiritual giant who so affected the world, offers us some profound wisdom when she says there should be less talk and more selfless action. Words not backed by action are simply "preaching points" and nothing more, but living a life in service to others both builds relationships and makes a statement about our values.

Behavior communicates volumes that words never can. I had always preached to people to be kind to animals, but my friend Pattie communicated this far more effectively than I ever had through her actions. Several years ago, I found a tiny squirrel that had been separated from its mother. While I was merely contemplating what we should do, Pattie didn't hesitate. She placed the squirrel in a shoebox, fed it, comforted it, and then called an animal shelter. Pattie drove that little squirrel to a shelter two hours away and refused to leave until she was assured no harm would come to it. Her actions taught me how real kindness and compassion for animals is supposed to be practiced.

Pattie, like Mother Theresa, knew that people of action—the doers in life—are the ones who make the greatest difference. More lives are changed by the influence of behavior than all the words in the dictionary could ever convey.

Marshall Foch

*"The most powerful weapon on earth
is the human soul on fire."*
—Marshall Foch (1851–1929)

The great French general of World War I knew that what wins wars is the spirit of its soldiers. Although high-tech weaponry and great fighting strategies may be important, what ultimately tips the scales in favor of victory is the passionate pursuit of cherished goals by the rank-and-file soldiers. We need only to look at modern-day examples of successful guerrilla wars (such as US vs. Vietnam or USSR vs. Afghanistan) to see the truth of this. Similarly, in our individual lives, when we have a worthy and consuming purpose, the passion generated is what carries us to personal triumph. When we really love what we do, we enjoy the entire journey toward our goals and are able to overcome any obstacles. So let's follow General Foch's wisdom and "Light 'em up!"

51.

Pierre Teilhard de Chardin

*"Someday, after we have mastered the winds,
the waves, the tide and gravity, we shall harness for
God the energies of love. Then, for the second time in
the history of the world, man will have discovered fire."*

—Pierre Teilhard de Chardin (1881–1955)

Pierre Teilhard de Chardin, the French-born Jesuit priest, shares the idea that if human beings were to fully practice loving kindness, our lives would be radically transformed—just as they were by the discovery of fire ages ago.

Despite tragic events in today's world, we can still choose to cultivate love. Researchers who have studied "mob psychology" know that the attitudes and actions of a few individuals can soon permeate an entire group, which then acts with increasingly greater power. A "mob" of loving people can harness this critical energy that will unite and revive our troubled world. We can all play our part to stoke the mighty fire of love.

Henry David Thoreau

"If a man does not keep pace with his
companions, perhaps it is because he
hears a different drummer. Let him step
to the music he hears, however
measured and far away."

—Henry David Thoreau (1817–1862)

Thoreau reminds us the music we hear internally is the connection to our soul's purpose. We must not ignore or suppress it in an attempt to conform to society. If we continue to ignore our inner drummer, we'll live a life of frustration. Whatever we feel compelled to be or do is the voice of our soul pleading with us to have the courage to listen and then to boldly act on the melody we hear. Thoreau's own life symbolizes this philosophy of following one's personal drumbeat while honoring other peoples' right to follow the music they hear—however strident and off-key it may sound to us.

53.

Anonymous

NEW FRIENDS AND OLD FRIENDS

Make new friends, but keep the old;
Those are silver, these are gold.
New-made friendships, like new wine,
Age will mellow and refine.
Friendships that have stood the test—
Time and change—are surely best;
Brow may wrinkle, hair grow gray;
Friendship never knows decay.
For 'mid old friends, tried and true,
Once more we our youth renew.
But old friends, alas! may die;
New friends must their place supply.
Cherish friendship in your breast—
New is good, but old is best;
Make new friends, but keep the old;
Those are silver, these are gold.

—Anonymous

Entering a new season is a wonderful time to reflect on the beauty and value of friendships, particularly the old ones. In our age, when casual acquaintance often comes so easily, we need to remember that genuine friendships were built over time. They took effort to make, and they take work to keep. Friendship is a deep thing, and indeed, a form of love. And while it may be, as C. S. Lewis said, the least biological form of love, it is still one of the most important. As we race off to chase this year's goals, let's not forget to nurture our friendships—especially those that are old—for they are the ones of Solid Gold.

54.

Patanjali

"When you are inspired by some great purpose, some extraordinary project, all your thoughts break their bonds; Your mind transcends limitations, your consciousness expands in every direction, and you find yourself in a new, great and wonderful world. Dormant forces, faculties and talents become alive, and you discover yourself to be a greater person by far than you ever dreamed yourself to be."
—Patanjali (circa 1st to 3rd Century B.C.)

Patanjali, considered by many the father of meditation, wrote more than 3,000 years ago about the incredible power of being inspired by an extraordinary endeavor or great purpose. Even those living in pre-pre-premodern times were aware of the importance of pursuing something significant for their lives. When we follow after something we absolutely love, our thoughts will be aligned with an energy beyond ourselves that will allow us to transcend a whole host of limitations.

As we become inspired, dormant forces, faculties, and talents are awakened within us, and we begin to manifest things we thought were outside our reach. We experience that state-of-being called "flow"—"a peak experience." You may have witnessed basketball players who slip into the "zone" and seem to score with every ball they throw toward the basket. You may have heard musicians whose improvisation takes their tune to new levels of creativity. I know there have been times when I've spoken before a crowd and have had words, humor, or entire teaching points pour right out of me, leaving me wondering where they had come from.

Call it what you will, it's hard for me to ascribe this experience to anything except divine providence. It is to be so entwined or caught up in your purpose that, for a period of time, it's almost impossible to separate yourself from it. I am convinced, like Patanjali was, that being inspired by a mighty purpose will allow every one of us to become a greater person than we ever dreamed possible.

55

John F. Kennedy

*"The problems of the world cannot be solved by
skeptics or cynics whose horizons are limited to
obvious realities. We need men and women who
can dream of things that never were."*

—John F. Kennedy (1917–1963)

Are you willing to dream? Are you willing to look at accomplishments that would stretch you beyond your present reality? Are you willing to pursue the goals that conventional wisdom tells you are unattainable or impossible? If you answered yes to these questions, you are destined for greatness—destined to live an extraordinary life and help create a better world.

Take a young boy, gazing at the stars and wondering if man would ever go there. Give him a challenging life, an engineering degree, a critical missed promotion in the aerospace industry, and you have Dan Goldin, former director for NASA. By forming alliances with Russia, Italy, Japan, and Germany, Goldin spearheaded the largest cooperative space exploration program ever undertaken by the human race.

We must dream of things that others cannot see and then find a way to share our vision, if we are ever going to change the world or our own lives. A teacher once passed out crayons and blank paper and told the children they could draw whatever they liked.

"What are you drawing?" he asked one child.

"A house."

"What are you making?" he asked another child.

"A snowman."

A third child was busy sketching, but the design was hard to figure out, so the teacher asked, "And what are you drawing?"

"Oh, I'm going to draw a picture of God," the child earnestly replied.

"How can you do that? No one knows what God looks like."

"They will when I'm done."

Living an extraordinary life that changes the world for the better requires a lot of hard work, but it begins with a dream—a dream of things that never were.

Leonardo da Vinci

"Every now and then go away, have a little relaxation,
for when you come back to your work your judgment
will be surer; since to remain constantly at work will
cause you to lose power of judgment . . ."

—Leonardo da Vinci (1452–1519)

Leonardo da Vinci has been hailed as having the most inquiring mind of all time and is considered by most historians as the original Renaissance man. His creativity and innovation are unparalleled, even today, and command us to listen closely when he stresses the importance of the Sabbath in our work lives. He advises us to distance ourselves from our work in order to become more productive when we return. His original (and now popular) message about the importance of balance tells us that to avoid being consumed by anything, we must walk away from it—even when we "have too much to do." I have witnessed this in my own life when it comes to speaking preparation or my writing. Even when I feel that I can't spare the time, if I leave my work to go for a long-distance run, or for deep meditation, I am amazed at how much clearer things are when I return. You can follow Leonardo's advice and bring balance into your life by stepping back from your work from time to time. In doing so, you'll gain a better perspective on your work and, ultimately, on your life!

57.

Robert Frost

> *"Two roads diverged in a wood, and I—*
> *I took the one less traveled by,*
> *and that has made all the difference."*
> —Robert Frost (1874–1963)

Robert Frost, writing of the road "less traveled by," speaks of something more transcendent than merely picking the less busy highway at a fork in the road. He is telling us that there are forks in the road of life where we'll only get one chance—and we must make that choice based on our instincts. Frost reminds us to be particularly wary of the road the rest of the pack seems to be following—the road "more traveled by." We must resist peer pressure and instead know that if we truly want to make a difference in life, we often must be willing to do things differently than the way everybody else does them. Frost himself was expected to be a farmer, a lawyer, and then a teacher. He left farming. He left law. He even left Harvard University to take the road less traveled— the road of becoming a poet. That decision has made all the difference! He gave the world extraordinary poetry, all because he followed his instincts at the fork in the road.

Orison Swett Marden

"Deep within man dwell those slumbering powers;
powers that would astonish him, that he never
dreamed of possessing; forces that would revolutionize
his life if aroused and put into action."
—Orison Swett Marden (1850–1924)

The powers within us must be awakened, wrote the founder of the American success movement, if we are going to transform our lives and live our dreams.

A lot of people don't see themselves as having anything vital or powerful within them. They cruise along based on their past experiences and limited awareness. People who live like this never use their talents and gifts to realize their greatness.

Have you heard the ancient fable of the little eagle that never aroused its slumbering powers?

Quite by accident, a farmer found an eagle's egg on a hill. He carried it to the chicken coop near his barn and plopped it alongside some eggs in the nest of a hen. Later, the eagle hatched among a brood of chicks.

As the eagle grew, it did what chickens do, since it was convinced it was a chicken. It clucked. It flapped its wings to fly a few feet in the air. Like the real chickens, it searched for no more exotic food than seed and insects.

One day the little eagle looked up into the sky and saw the most dazzling creature it had ever seen.

"What is that?" it asked, startled by the sheer majesty of the form soaring gracefully in wide circles in and out of the high clouds.

"That," a rooster said in a hushed, reverent tone, "is an eagle, the greatest of all birds."

"Wow, I'd like to do that!"

"Forget it," the rooster advised. "We're chickens."

Do you recognize the little eagle who thought it was a chicken? Sometimes that's us, isn't it? If we want to experience the heights to which we can soar, we have to awaken our slumbering powers within and press them into action. We don't want to be too "chicken" to grab hold of our greatness!

59

Zig Ziglar and
Bryant S. Hinckley

*"You can get everything in life you want if you just
help enough other people get what they want."*

—Zig Ziglar

*"Service is the virtue that distinguished the great of all times
and which they will be remembered by. It places a mark of
nobility upon its disciples. It is the dividing line which sepa-
rates the two great groups of the world—those who help and
those who hinder, those who lift and those who lean, those
who contribute and those who only consume. How much better
it is to give than receive. Service in any form is comely and
beautiful. To give encouragement, to impart sympathy, to show
interest, to banish fear, to build self-confidence and awaken
hope in the hearts of others, in short—to love them and to
show it—is to render the most precious service."*

—Bryant S. Hinckley, author of *Not by Bread Alone*

One of the world's most famous men has been a role model
for serving others. In 1982 Paul Newman started a food
company called "Newman's Own." Since then he has poured more
than $100 million of profits into hundreds of charities. Newman
also started a camp for kids diagnosed with cancer. Periodically he
visited the camp and stationed himself at a little lemonade stand
and poured lemonade for these desperately sick children. When
asked by a journalist why he did that, he shrugged and said, "Well,

I guess because I love doing it." It sounds to me that writing charity checks and pouring lemonade for enough others expanded Paul's heart and gave him more in return than he could ever imagine.

There's an intrinsic security and fulfillment that comes by providing service, by helping other people in a meaningful way. One important way is our work, when we see ourselves in a creative and contributive mode, really making a difference. Another source is anonymous service—the service no one ever needs to know about—but is based on serving and blessing the lives of others. Influence, and not recognition, becomes the motive. The late Dr. Hans Selye, in his groundbreaking research on stress, says that a long, healthy, and happy life is the result of making contributions and blessing the lives of others. His ethic was "earn thy neighbor's love."

N. Eldon Tanner said, "Service is the rent we pay for the privilege of living on this earth." There are so many ways to serve. Whether we belong to a church or service organization or have a job that provides meaningful service, not a day goes by that we can't serve at least one other human being by demonstrating unconditional love though our behavior.

60

George Ludwig

*"I have come to believe that an unopened gift
is a tragedy. Every human being is born with
unique gifts, but, unbelievably, most people never
open theirs. My mission in life is to help people take
the wraps off and see what they're really capable of."*

—George Ludwig

The holiday season provides a great metaphor for reminding us that we must open our gifts if we want to lead happy, fulfilled lives. If we unwrap our unique talents and develop them fully, we have the opportunity to reach our maximum potential as human beings.

Imagine giving your child a unique gift for their birthday or for Christmas. You picked a gift especially for them. You took into account all you knew about them and were very proud of how well it matched their wants and needs. Then at Christmas, they refused to open it. Or if they opened it, they never used it. Or maybe they did open it, but never read the directions on how to have the most fun with it.

I imagine that the Creator, or Supreme Being, or whatever you happen to call that Higher Power feels disappointed and sad when we do not open, develop, and bring our gifts out for all the world to experience and enjoy.

There's a little fable about a Mr. Smith who dies and goes to heaven. St. Peter is waiting at the gates to give him a tour. Amid the splendor of the golden streets, beautiful mansions, and Angel guides that St. Peter shows him, Mr. Smith notices an odd-looking building. He thinks it looks like an enormous warehouse—it has no windows and only one door. But when he wants to look inside, St. Peter hesitates. "You really do not want to go in there," he tells the recent arrival. The newcomer persists, so St. Peter finally relents.

When the apostle opens the door, Mr. Smith almost knocks him over to see what's inside. It turns out that the enormous building is filled with row after row of shelves, floor to ceiling, each stacked neatly with white boxes tied with a red ribbon. Each box has a name on it. Then turning to St. Peter, Mr. Smith asks, "Do I have one?"

"Yes, you do." St. Peter tries to guide Mr. Smith back outside. Before St. Peter can get Mr. Smith back outside, Mr. Smith has already found the "S" aisle and is closing in on his own box. Mr. Smith finds his box, unties the red ribbon, and pops the lid. Looking inside, Mr. Smith has a moment of instant recognition, and then lets out a deep sigh like the ones St. Peter has heard so many times before.

Inside Mr. Smith's white box was an image of himself as God had intended him to be—an image in which he had developed and used all the gifts he had been given. His box held the Mr. Smith that could have been, but wasn't, the Mr. Smith that knew the deep fulfillment that comes with being who he was designed to be.

EPILOGUE

Thank you for reading this book. Now open the book to any one of the 60 tips and commit to do what's written. You'll be making a very *Wise Move* to improve your position in life or business.

I hope your hunt for wisdom and human excellence is fruitful and never-ending. My wish is that you enjoy much success, fulfillment, abundance, and happiness. And, I hope we get to meet someday soon, but until then—may God hold you gently in the palm of His hand.

Good-bye and many blessings.

ABOUT THE AUTHOR

George Ludwig is one of the nation's leaders in personal development training. He is the founder and president of GLU, a research, training, and development firm whose clients include Johnson & Johnson, Sprint, Mazda, Northwestern Mutual, Coldwell Banker, Southwest Airlines, and many other companies.

Since 1997, tens of thousands of people have enjoyed the warmth, humor, and dynamic presentation style of Mr. Ludwig's peak performance and sales success seminars. He has consulted and coached people from every walk of life. Ludwig has been quoted in *Time, Entrepreneur, Selling Power, Sales & Marketing Management,* and *The New York Times.*

Mr. Ludwig lives along the Fox River, near Chicago, Illinois.

GEORGE LUDWIG UNLIMITED

Resources for Personal Success

- Fast-Track Educational TeleSeminars℠
- Rapid Results Personal Coaching Systems℠
- Books & e-books
- Audio Programs

Resources for Organizational Success

- Sales Success Training
- Peak Performance & Personal Development Training
- Customized Speaking Presentations
- "Best Practices" and Process Development Consulting

For more information on any of the products and services offered by George Ludwig Unlimited, visit **www.georgeludwig.com**, call 888-999-4811, or write George Ludwig Unlimited, 2515 Grove Lane, Suite 100, Cary, IL 60013-2742.